How To Build

A Better

Business Plan

A Hands-On Action Guide for Business Owners

By Alastair Thomson

Legal Notices

The Action Guide is covered by the laws of copyright, which means it cannot be duplicated, copied, or distributed without permission of the copyright owner.

You should always seek appropriate professional advice, tailored to your personal circumstances, before making investments or embarking on any new business venture.

No warranties or guarantees are given or should be implied by this publication. Results will vary, depending on your individual expertise, background, experience, and the amount of hard work you invest.

The right of Alastair Thomson to be identified as the author of this work has been asserted by him in accordance with the Copyright, Designs and Patents Act 1988.

All rights reserved.

Table of Contents

Why you need a business plan

There's an old saying - if you don't know where you're going, any road will take you there.

If you're out for a leisurely hike through the country that might not matter too much (as long as you have a map and compass).

But if you try to run your business like that, I can virtually guarantee you won't arrive at a destination anywhere close to the one you were trying to reach.

What happens, over time, is that your business veers further and further off-course and you end up working harder and harder just to try and get it focused back on the target you had originally set.

Because it happens little by little, day by day, often business owners don't notice how far off-course their business has got until they wake up one morning and realize they've fallen out of love with the business which used to represent their passions, their hopes for the future, and their dreams of making an impact on the world.

Now, the business may well still be profitable and pay the bills. But if you have been a business owner for any length of time, you know that if your heart is not in your business, sooner or later you'll kill your business, or your business will kill you.

But it doesn't have to be that way.

That's where a good business plan comes in.

The good news

With a good business plan in place, you're no longer wandering aimlessly like a lost hiker trying to find the road back to civilization before they get eaten by wild bears.

You know exactly where you're going, how you're going to get there and how to keep your business on the right path to achieve every ambition you ever had for it.

You have planned ahead, so you know exactly what needs to happen to build the business of your dreams. Now you can throw all your energies into making that happen as fast as possible without being distracted or getting stuck up blind alleys.

Of course, from time-to-time people and events both inside and outside your business will knock you off your intended path for a while, no matter how hard you try to prevent that from happening.

However, if you follow the process in this Action Guide, you will spot any slippage straight away. That means you can get back on track quickly while it is still relatively cheap and simple to do so.

Without exception, the longer you leave any business problem, the more expensive it is to put right and the greater the risk you will never be able to get your business fully back on track again as one problem compounds on another, which makes unpicking them a thousand times harder.

The late Jim Rohn used to say achieving your objectives is like a pilot setting the autopilot for a cross-country flight.

If a pilot takes off, points the airplane's nose towards its destination, and takes their hands off the controls, successive gusts of wind during the flight would blow their aircraft further and further off-course. The passengers would never reach their destination.

If the pilot held their controls absolutely rigid, all the passengers would get airsick. The airplane would be changing direction several times a second as the pilot battled constantly to keep the airplane locked rigidly on course as each gust of wind came along.

By contrast, autopilots work by allowing a small amount of drift before they gently move the nose of the airplane back to the correct compass heading for their destination.

By definition, as Jim Rohn used to point out, the airplane was "off course" 95% of the time it flew on autopilot, although it always reached the destination it was supposed to.

What mattered was not that gusts of wind came along to blow the flight off-course. That happened on every flight. Rather, it was making sure there was a system in place to bring it gently back on course again without making everyone airsick in the process.

Your business is the same. With clarity of purpose and the right business plan in place, you will make it to your destination just fine.

When something happens to blow you off-course, don't ignore it but don't panic and hold onto the controls for dear life either. Just keep flying steady and let the autopilot nudge you back on course every so often to make sure you reach your intended destination.

Your business plan is like an autopilot for your business – you program in the destination and map out the stops along the way.

Then you just need to let your business plan do its job.

With the right business plan...

With the right business plan in place, you have a firm handle on:

- The best customers for your business and how to find them

- How to generate the sales revenue you need

- Your cost base – people costs, material costs and bought-in services

- Any investments in plant and equipment required to help your business grow faster and serve your customers better, and

- The finance you need realise your dreams

Not only that, you will also:

- Identify potential challenges along the way

- Spot new opportunities

- Understand when you need to reinvest and when you can safely take money out your business

- See trouble coming from a long way off, and

- Know exactly what to do if things don't go according to plan

With the right business plan, there is no more humming and hawing, wondering if you are headed in the right direction.

No more second-guessing when parents, partners, friends, and family express well-meaning concerns about your plans.

And no more financial or operational worries because you have worked those issues through carefully in advance, and you know you have developed a model that works.

Instead, you can press ahead with confidence because you're building your business on the solid foundations of a good business plan.

But do I *have* to?

I admit the expression "business plan" doesn't usually fill people with joy. It's one of those tasks businesspeople often avoid unless they're forced to write one.

Particularly in small-to-medium sized businesses, the main time the subject of writing a business plan comes up is when the business needs additional external funding, whether that's from an equity investor looking to put some money into your business in return for a percentage of the shares, or a provider of debt finance, like a bank.

Some investors and lenders will also expect you to prepare, and share with them, an annual business plan as a condition of continuing to fund your business.

That is not as unreasonable as it might first appear. Every equity investor wants to know the business will be more valuable in the future than it is today because that's how they make a profit on their investment.

And every bank or other lender wants to know they will get their money back in full at the end of the loan term.

For both investors and lenders, a business plan is of course invaluable for making those judgements before an equity investment is approved or the heads of terms on a loan agreement are signed. And a business plan is no less valuable on an ongoing basis during the lifetime of their relationship with your business.

After all, investors and lenders want to know their investment is safe and your business is on track to achieve what you promised them.

And, let's face it, you and I would want exactly the same if we were putting a substantial amount of money into a business we had no day-to-day control over.

That's how, often very reluctantly, many small and medium-sized businesses end up preparing a business plan for the first time.

They have avoided doing one for years, but when investors and lenders insist on seeing a business plan before they agree to buy a percentage of the business or approve a new lending facility, business owners don't have a choice.

Unfortunately, as a result of them only setting about this task because they were told they had to, business owners don't always approach the process with the level of enthusiasm which generates the biggest benefits from the business planning process.

Admittedly, that is better than not planning at all but still, that lack of motivation can mean business owners miss out on the greatest benefits of preparing a business plan.

You see, a business plan isn't...or, at least, shouldn't be...a dull, pointless exercise which is only done to convince an investor or lender to hand over their cash.

A business plan is, in fact, your roadmap for success. And who wouldn't want one of those?

The real benefits of a business plan

Yes, a good business plan will get you the funding you need.

But other benefits of a good business plan are many times greater than any benefit funding alone might bring.

For example, you get to consider your business from several different perspectives and make sure it is built in the best possible way to get where you want to go.

You develop a deeper understanding of where your business is potentially vulnerable – perhaps a single customer accounts for a large proportion of your sales, or a critical component of your product or service is highly sensitive to short-notice price spikes – and you have the opportunity to put a plan in place to counteract that now, at a time of relative peace and calm, rather than waiting to see if the worst happens and hoping you can figure something out on the fly if it does.

A good business plan is not just about protecting your downside, though. You also get to uncover opportunities which could increase your revenues and reduce your costs, helping your business grow faster and make more money.

That's why, whether or not you're looking for external funding or investment, the discipline of doing a business plan at least once a year is always worthwhile.

But that's not all.

With a business plan, you also have a great resource to communicate with.

Whether you're communicating with new members of staff, customers, key suppliers or the media, a business plan helps you get clear about where you're headed. You communicate with confidence and passion because you know what your future looks like and how you're going to get there.

For new hires, existing staff, customers, suppliers, and the media alike, that can be intoxicating in a world where so many businesses just drift along.

Even if they never see the full document, your staff, your customers, and your key suppliers sense you know what you're doing, and you know where you're headed. That is a very attractive quality in any business owner...and rarer than you might think.

You see, your business plan doesn't just record something you believe in. It also gives other people something to buy into.

Finally, it is amazing how often just knowing what you're trying to do makes something more likely to happen.

Once you get complete clarity about what you want, your brain, subconsciously, starts to look for ways to make that happen for you.

All of a sudden, for reasons you can't quite explain, you'll drive past a place you've driven past hundreds of times before and spot something you never noticed up till now which proves to be the seed of a huge business opportunity.

You'll bump into someone at a networking event and have the same sort of conversation over a cup of coffee you've had hundreds of times before, except this time your brain picks out something they say which opens the door to a whole new set of opportunities you would never have imagined.

Or you'll be idly leafing through a magazine or browsing the internet and see a headline which makes you think "I wonder if that could help me achieve my business ambitions".

That's why, in addition to the tangible benefit of unlocking the financial support you need, an annual business plan brings a whole range of valuable, but perhaps less obvious, benefits too.

Unlocking the financial support you need might be a good enough reason to prepare a business plan the first time.

But it's not a coincidence that people who know where they're going and how they're going to get there tend to get where they're headed faster, and with less hassle, than people who just set out hoping for the best.

By preparing an annual business plan, you become one of those people who know where they're going and how they're going to get there. You dramatically increase the odds of achieving bigger and better ambitions for your business more quickly and more smoothly than you could ever have imagined.

Let's get started.

Some helpful resources

Writing a business plan can seem daunting at first. Of course, if you follow the steps in this Action Guide it will be a lot less daunting than it would otherwise be, but sometimes a bit of extra support can come in handy.

The good news is that, because you purchased this book, you can download your own free business planning template as a Word document to customise and tailor for your own business needs.

All the sections mirror the chapters in this Action Guide, so you can complete each section of your own business plan as you follow along.

And it has all the "must have" elements from each section of this Action Guide to make sure you leave nothing out and you capitalise on every opportunity.

You can download your free business plan template here:

www.TheBetterBusinessCompany.com/BPtemplate

You can also get a range of coaching solutions to support you on the path to writing a business plan which attracts the financial support you need to kick-start the process of achieving your business dreams.

Coaching support is available either for the entire end-to-end process of creating your own business plan, or on an "as needed" basis for specific support on one of the individual sections.

Full details of the coaching support available is here:

www.TheBetterBusinessCompany.com/BPcoach

Before you start

Business owners tend to fall into one of two categories when it comes to business planning.

(Well, one of three categories, technically, but if you have made it this far, I'm working on the assumption you don't, mistakenly, believe all business planning is a waste of time and the prime role of a business owner is to swashbuckle through life like a latter-day Douglas Fairbanks.)

Swashbucklers aside, business owners tend to be either wildly over-optimistic or wildly over-pessimistic when it comes to assessing the future prospects for their business.

Neither is good or bad but, when it comes to business planning, it is important to understand which you are for one simple reason.

That knowledge gives you a powerful starting point for assessing the risks and opportunities for your business in a way that many business owners never get round to doing.

So, if you do, you stand a much better chance of outmanoeuvring your competitors when the world doesn't go exactly according to plan which, sooner or later, it is almost certain to do.

The 1 – 2 – 3 Method

A good approach to building a business plan which delivers results, as well as demonstrating to investors and lenders that you have thought through the key issues affecting your business, is to develop three versions of your business plan – a best-case scenario where everything goes swimmingly, a worst-case version with some big challenges along the way, and a "likely outcome" somewhere in the middle.

Don't panic – this doesn't need to be a long, complex, expensive exercise, as you'll see later. But for now, let's focus on the benefits of creating your business plan this way.

To give a simple example, if you expect to make sales of $100,000 a week, you might run the numbers for sales of $120,000 a week and $80,000 a week to see what impact fluctuations in your sales, either up or down, might have on your business.

Often, business owners worry about what they will do if sales come in lower than expected. And it's fair to say it's always helpful to consider what options you would have to manage your cost base if that was to happen.

But it's also important to look deeper than that and not just take those lower sales numbers as a given.

Perhaps you should take a closer look at your sales model – for example, when you look a little closer, maybe it turns out you are getting as many leads as you used to get, but whereas you used to convert one lead in three into a sale, now you're only converting 1-in-5.

In that situation, it is much more important to prioritise fixing your sales model over randomly cutting costs. Too much cost-cutting could leave you exposed when your sales model gets back on track and volumes jump back up again.

There is no feeling quite as bad as making a sale but missing out on a nice chunk of profit because you took a short-term cost-saving decision which removed your ability to deliver to the client's specification and timescale.

Important though it is to consider the impact of bad news, many business owners forget to consider what they would do if sales come in much higher than expected.

Your customers might start to experience quality or delivery issues as the pressure ramps up on your workforce. There might not be enough people on the ground to keep service, quality, and delivery on track.

With the right business plan, you do your thinking up-front. You know how to take advantage when new opportunities come your way and you know exactly what problem needs solving if performance veers off-course.

That's a good thing because, as the business owner, both at times of great challenge and times of great opportunity, you need to keep a clear head even if everyone around you is panicking.

People with clear heads who know where they're going and how they're going to get there tend to make much better decisions in the middle of a crisis than those who don't.

It's not as crazy as it sounds

The great advantage of the 1-2-3 Method is that you can scenario-plan some options up-front to give you a clear idea of the alternatives which might be open to you should either opportunities or challenges come your way. No business plan can predict the future perfectly.

If all this sounds a bit over-the-top, it is worth remembering the armed forces, paramedics, firefighters, and airline pilots, among many other professions, run drills under a wide range of different potential situations all the time.

In the heat of battle, or if one of an airliner's two jet engines stops working mid-Atlantic, the professionals at the sharp end of a crisis do not need to waste valuable time assessing potential options, wondering what data they might need, or what action they should take.

They have already trained for a range of different possible options including, in all likelihood, the exact situation they're facing at that moment or something very close to it.

Remember Captain "Sully" Sullenberger? He landed his fully loaded Airbus A320 on the Hudson River in New York, soon after taking off from La Guardia Airport, when a flock of Canada Geese took out both engines.

The prompt, calm actions of Captain Sullenberger saved the lives of his 155 passengers.

It was no coincidence he had spent hours in the Airbus simulator preparing himself for all manner of major incidents, including having to ditch his airplane on water.

That's what professional pilots do as a matter of course. They never stop practicing. They work through hundreds of different scenarios in the simulator before ever being called upon to do it "for real", so they are primed for action no matter what happens.

For most of us, running a business isn't like hand-to-hand combat in a war zone, or having both engines blow out on an Airbus jet we're piloting...or at least it shouldn't be.

But the same principle applies. Your business is just as mission-critical to you as the work of the fine professionals in our armed forces, the healthcare sector and the airline industry is to them and the people they care for.

Any business owner can learn a lot by copying this example and working through a range of options long before they have to deal with a major crisis erupting out of nowhere without warning.

That way, you are fully prepared when the unexpected happens. And if there is one thing I can assure you about the business world, it's that the unexpected will most definitely happen from time to time.

More importantly, whatever happens, you will be able to respond straight away because you took the time to think through what you would do if, for example, 20% of your sales disappeared overnight, rather than wasting valuable time in the middle of a full-blown crisis, wondering what options you have and being under pressure to conjure up a response on the hoof.

Are you an optimist or a pessimist?

Why does it matter for your business plan to know whether you are one of life's boundless optimists or one of life's natural pessimists?

Well, if you are one of life's optimists, your initial thoughts for your business plan are likely to somewhat on the optimistic side too.

Thinking back to the 1-2-3 Method, you need to consider how you might step down from your initial thoughts to a more balanced assessment of what a likely outcome might be, and then step down again from there to imagine what a worst-case scenario could look like.

To link it back to the example earlier in this section, an optimist's first run-through of their business plan is likely to be for weekly sales of $120,000 because they have trouble imagining everything not going completely according to plan.

If that's you, then you need to work out how you would run your business differently if sales were only $100,000...or even as low as $80,000.

The biggest danger for an optimist is having a cost base which is too high, buoyed by an overly optimistic outlook for the future. This leaves the business badly exposed if the ambitious sales targets don't come to fruition.

This isn't "doubting your ability" or "undermining your confidence", as I sometimes hear business owners describe looking at the possibility of anything other than perfect outcomes.

Rather, this approach is about considering possible alternative scenarios and taking sensible precautions to make sure, whatever happens, you have a strategy to tackle any challenges head-on and still come out on top.

I have seen over-optimism destroy many a fine business because the business owner could not begin to conceive of the world not going completely according to plan. Do not let that be you.

Equally, a pessimist's first run-through a business plan is likely to lead them naturally to the worst-case scenario. If that sounds like you, then you need to step up twice from your initial thoughts to get the full range of options.

Going back to the example from the start of this section, you are likely to have started with the $80,000 weekly sales figure, so you need to consider what you would do differently if sales came in at $100,000 or even $120,000 a week instead.

The biggest danger for a pessimist is under-resourcing their business. Because of a low sales number, they tend to cut business costs to the bone.

That might seem like a good move, but if sales come in any higher than you thought, your people will quickly get overwhelmed and you run the risk of letting customers down badly on service, quality and delivery (or all three).

This in turn leads to poor customer feedback and a reputation for letting customers down which hampers future growth opportunities. Nobody wants to deal with an unreliable supplier.

Remember there is no judgement here. There is nothing wrong with being either an optimist or a pessimist as long as you know which you are and prepare accordingly.

In any business there will inevitably be times when the unexpected happens.

All you need to do is make sure you spend enough time in the simulator so that, like Captain Sullenberger, you can land your plane safely and save everyone on board should the unexpected happen.

"I'm straight down the middle"

Don't convince yourself for a moment that you're one of those "straight down the middle" people. Very few people are…so few, in fact, that I can virtually guarantee you are not one of them.

Every optimist I ever met was completely convinced their projections were "incredibly conservative". Every pessimist I ever met was just as firmly convinced they were "only being realistic".

We all have blind spots, so try asking some friends, colleagues, business contacts or family members for some feedback. Just don't take what they say at face value – at some level they will err on the side of politeness, especially if they are an employee, a friend, or a family member.

"You set ambitious targets" means they see you as a wild-eyed optimist.

"You're always very realistic" means you are the most conservative person they know.

"I'd say you were somewhere in the middle" means they are too polite to upset you, but secretly suspect you're strongly one or the other.

Whatever third parties tell you, corroborate what they say by looking back at your past results – do you set yourself tough targets and then beat yourself up for not achieving them? If you do, you're an optimist.

Or do you constantly worry about your business, lie awake at night, and wonder how you'll ever meet this month's payroll, yet remarkably always deliver the bottom line you set out to deliver? If that sounds like you, then you're a pessimist.

Calibrating where you're starting from before you begin to work through the impact of external events, both good and bad, on your business is a powerful way to develop a business plan with the right amount of stretch and challenge.

Not so much it becomes "pie in the sky". Not so little that you never quite reach your full potential because you were overly cautious and didn't push yourself and your team hard enough.

Neither optimism nor pessimism is a barrier to creating a great business. But not knowing which of the two you are often can be. One way or another, usually without realizing it, you can end up sabotaging your own success.

The do-over

Once you have calibrated your outlook on life, you can work through this Action Guide with that perspective in mind, whether you're one of life's sunny-spirited optimists or someone who has no trouble thinking of 100 potential downsides for every upside that comes their way.

Having done that, though, there is one more outcome you need to accept – the possibility that, after you work through your business plan right to the end, and despite a lot of hard work on your part, it becomes clear your business plan doesn't work out financially.

It might sound odd to mention that up-front in a book about business planning, but that's the whole point of business planning. This is a great result, not a failure.

The output from the business planning process isn't just "a plan".

The only output that matters from a business planning process is finding a business model that works, one which generates the profits and cash flow you need to achieve your ambitions. Your business plan document is just a way for you to record what that model is.

As Thomas Edison said, after trying 10,000 different ways to make an electric lightbulb, he didn't fail 10,000 times, he successfully found 10,000 ways which didn't work.

So, don't be disheartened if your first pass doesn't bring the "happy ever after" story you hoped for.

It is much better to realise a business plan won't work on paper when all you've invested is a few hours of your time, than to invest six or seven figures in cold, hard cash in a business only to lose it all when the real world gives you the brutal feedback that your plan isn't financially viable.

If your first attempt doesn't work out as well as you hoped financially, just shrug your shoulders, refine your ideas and work through the process one more time.

The difference is this time you will know exactly what threw you off course on the first pass. Odds are it will only be one or two key metrics which caused the problem. Fix those and everything will work perfectly.

That's the real power of business planning.

If the numbers show that to make a profit you would need to sell more dinners every night than the number of people who live within a reasonable travel radius of your restaurant, it's a clear sign you need to think again.

If your selling price is so low that you can't invest in the equipment you need to run your business, it's a clear sign you need to take a closer look at that selling price and see how you can charge more.

If the fixed costs of running your business (rent, utilities, salaries, etc) are so high that they wipe out your gross margin on sales, it's a clear sign you need to take another look at your fixed costs, your selling prices, your gross margins, or all three.

Let's get started

With the right business plan in place, you'll spot where the critical issues are before you need to make your plan work in the real world.

That way, you can fix problems before they happen, rather than being taken by surprise and having to put things right again somewhere down the line, usually at much greater expense than it would have cost to fix them up-front.

And, just as important, you get to anticipate what to do when things go really well.

Many business owners worry about things going badly. They forget that many otherwise fine businesses get overwhelmed because they couldn't respond effectively to an amazing opportunity.

They over-reached, and instead of the fairy tale story they hoped for, ended up losing everything on the back of what should have been a great success (a major contract win, prominent press coverage, a viral social media post, and so on).

Sometimes great opportunities arriving unexpectedly in your lap can lead to more challenges for your business than the hard times, with the added dimension that everyone, including you, is under immense pressure to get things right at a time of unprecedented activity.

So be like those armed forces personnel, healthcare professionals and airline pilots who consider what challenging situations they might encounter and practice what they would do in a simulator far away from the front line long before they need to take any decisions under fire in the middle of a crisis.

While you're about it, don't forget to share your scenario planning with your investors and lenders. (There's a whole section about how to do that towards the end of this Action Guide.)

That way, you give investors and lenders confidence they're dealing with a smart professional who knows what they're doing and has prepared as well as anyone could for any challenges which might come their way.

Enough of the preamble. Let's start building your business plan together, one section at a time.

Our first port of call is the Executive Summary.

Executive Summary: Setting the tone

Your business plan should always start with an executive summary.

At least, that is the first section investors and lenders should see when they open up your business plan document. But here's a bit of an insider tip – it's probably the section you should leave till last to complete.

By all means map out some of the headings and drop in a key fact or two. But it is generally easier to write the rest of the plan first, and then come back to this section once you've developed the level of clarity you need on all the finer points of your business plan – how you're going to organise your marketing, your product profitability, your financing needs, and so on.

That way, you will be able to pick out all the stats you need from the relevant sections of the business plan, you'll be enthused about the wonderful prospects you've uncovered for your business, and you'll be in the right frame of mind to make sure your Executive Summary hits investors and lenders with the impact it needs when they open the front cover and start to read.

Because your Executive Summary is the first section lenders or investors read, you need to start out strongly. Don't leave first impressions to chance – their first impressions need to be positive impressions.

But, however interested and excited you are about them, don't dive straight into a barrage of details right from the off and leave investors and lenders to find their own way through without your steady hand on the tiller to point them in the right direction.

Not teeing up your business plan properly through your Executive Summary will just confuse and irritate investors and lenders. And you run the risk of coming across as unstructured and unclear in your thinking, which is definitely not a good first impression for investors and lenders to form.

The Executive Summary is where you take the opportunity to set the stage and help readers quickly understand your business, your goals, your ambitions, and your financing needs.

It's where you're going to trail your "coming attractions" in the rest of your business plan document. And it's where you're going to start engaging and exciting investors and lenders about the great opportunities ahead for them if they give you the support you need now.

There's time to fill in the details later. The Executive Summary section is a 'helicopter view' of the broad strategic direction of your business.

It's also where you want to get emotional buy-in from investors and lenders. You shape their perceptions of your entire business plan by what you say - and don't say - in this section.

A brilliant Executive Summary sets you firmly on the path for success, with your readers rooting for you right out the starting gate.

By the same token, no matter how good the rest of your business plan is, if the first impression you give investors and lenders isn't engaging enough, you'll have a mountain to climb in the rest of the business plan document to recover.

A good Executive Summary is your first step on the path to success.

Like an elevator pitch

Think of your Executive Summary as the business plan equivalent of an elevator pitch.

A good Executive Summary should give investors and lenders a general sense of what your business is all about, the products and services you sell, where your business has been and where it's headed.

By the time they have read your Executive Summary, you want investors and lenders to be silently rooting for you. You want to get them on your side from the start and excited enough about the prospects for your business to want to read more.

That I s especially important because what very few people will tell you is the Executive Summary might be the only section of your business plan which gets read.

Professionals, like bankers and investors, do not read business plans from start to finish like novels, devouring every detail. Maybe they should, but they don't.

They're busy people with hundreds of business plans to plough through every year, so they need some way to sort the wheat from the chaff, some way to spot the diamonds in the rough.

In practice, investors and lenders often read the Executive Summary to get the gist of the proposal and decide if it excites them enough to read further.

If they like the broad concepts in your Executive Summary, and you get them on your side, then...and only then...they might take a quick look at the financial numbers towards the end of your business plan document.

Finally, if your proposal passes muster on the financial front, they will go back to the start of your plan and read it through from front to back in order to fill in more of the details they need to make an investment decision.

But it's most definitely that way round.

If they are not excited by your Executive Summary on page 2, odds are investors and lenders are not going to keep reading on the off chance you're going to blow them away with a brilliant insight on page 97.

If you don't grab your audience's attention with the Executive Summary, the most likely outcome is they won't read the rest of your business plan at all.

That's why, although it will contain some factual information, your Executive Summary needs to leave potential investors and lenders enthusiastic about your business and eager to get involved.

If your Executive Summary is compelling enough and exciting enough, people will read the rest of your business plan to find the factual information they require to make an investment decision.

But if they're bored, confused, or actively turned off by your Executive Summary, the chances of them reading a single word of the rest of your business plan are extremely low.

It's not all about the numbers

I know it's tempting to think business plans are all about numbers and finance. But that's not true at all.

The purpose of a good business plan is to help lenders and investors understand they have an exciting prospect on their hands. That goes double in the Executive Summary section.

While the numbers are important, and they will be used by investors and lenders in their investment appraisal calculations, think of it like buying a new car purely on the basis of its top speed or its fuel consumption.

Nobody chooses a new car on that basis. At least, not unless you're the sort of person who would buy a Formula 1 car for millions of dollars because it's got the highest top speed without stopping to realise you can't fit the family in there with you and there's no room for your golf clubs.

Instead, we get swept away with imagining how having that particular model parked up on our driveway would make us feel about ourselves.

Or we think about the logistics of having to fit four kids under 8 years old in the back with all their sports equipment.

Or we choose a vehicle we would be happy to let our teenage daughter learn to drive in without worrying she might get pulled for speeding or attract unwelcome attention.

We all buy cars for reasons which have absolutely nothing to do with the numbers and statistics.

It's not until quite some way through the process of deciding which car to buy...often not until we've narrowed our choice down to two or three potential options...that we start asking questions about the mileage it gets or how much a new set of tires would cost.

The same is true for your business plan.

Make sure your head is firmly in marketing mode, rather than in finance mode, for your Executive Summary. You are doing the equivalent of persuading investors and lenders to imagine how tantalising your shiny new model car would look on their driveway long before they have a test drive or enquire about the finance options.

Topics investors and lenders expect to see in your Executive Summary include:

- Mission statement
  A short (one paragraph) summary of your business and the big picture goals you're pursuing. This isn't one of those dreadful "Helping make the world a better place through advanced technology solutions" sort of mission statements. That doesn't get you funding, it just gets you an eye roll.

  Be clear about your purpose, who you sell to, the markets you serve and the way you serve them. That is the most important information potential investors and lenders need up-front as that will frame how they read the rest of your document. Make this clear and compelling.

- Legal structure and ownership
  This includes the founding date of your business, names and roles of your founders and any other key snippets of information which might help give an idea of the size and scale of your business, such as how many employees you have or the number of locations you operate from (if you have more than one).

  Don't get into the detail – there's plenty of scope that later. "Formed in 2012 by the current management team…" is more than enough. This isn't the place for life stories or mini resumes.

- Company highlights
  Draw attention to important moments in your company history - financial milestones, major contract wins, significant awards, and

other important events on your journey so far. If you are just getting started, include information from past ventures to help build the credibility you need with investors and lenders.

- Products and services
  A short description of what you sell and who your customers are (or what they will be if your product or service is still under development).

- Financial information
  If you are looking for funding, you will need to spell out both your financing goals as well as any sources of funding that you may already have in place, including the headroom on any unused facilities.

- Future plans
  While all of the Executive Summary section should be considered a sales proposal for investors and lenders, this section should be considered the sales proposal of all sales proposals.

  Up to now, you have been trying to convince investors and lenders you have the track record necessary to run a successful business using their money. Now you need to build a bridge from your successful past to the exciting future they can be part of if they decide to support you now.

While some of this information will be factual, professional investors and lenders who review business plans for a living know they will be able to find all the facts they need elsewhere in your document.

At this point you should primarily be conveying the excitement of what your business can achieve in the future. That is vital for potential investors and lenders as this is how they improve the chances of a big payday for themselves in the not-too-distant future.

Without being too blatant, you're trying to sell them on the opportunity. You're trying to engage them, in the same way you'd look to engage a major sales prospect. You're trying to get them enthusiastic about becoming a key part of your business's exciting future and making a great financial return for themselves in the process.

If your Executive Summary doesn't do those things, don't be too surprised if they pass.

This is where you want to make sure your business, and its prospects for the future, shine!

Cover all the bases

Whatever happens, make sure you cover all the bases. Even the bits you might prefer not to.

Investors and lenders see dozens of business plans each week, so they develop a nose for things that don't feel quite right.

It's like the Sherlock Homes story "The Hound of the Baskervilles" in which the famous fictional sleuth's biggest insight was that the guard dogs didn't bark at the intruder, which had to mean the guilty party was someone the dogs already knew.

Same goes for investors and lenders. If something they expect to see isn't there, they will think you're either trying to hide something or they will wonder if you have the level of insight they would normally expect from business leaders they invest in.

That's never a good starting point.

Even in areas where you are not as confident as you would ideally like to be, or even where things are frankly pretty unflattering, make sure you cover the topic in your business plan and explain what you're doing about it.

Maybe there's a key hire you haven't found yet. Don't gloss over it. Just explain what the gap is and what you're doing to fill it.

Maybe you have applied for a trademark or patent but have not yet had the formal registration approved. Explain where you are in the process, what steps remain and why you are confident that, ultimately, you will get the intellectual property protection you need for your business.

Maybe your funding proposal is to help you get out from under a historic situation where you've had the bad end of a deal, like an onerous lease or a supply contract on punitive terms.

Don't be embarrassed about past mistakes.

Investors and lenders are vastly more impressed by someone who has spotted the error of their ways, owns up to them and is actively doing something to make things better than they are by someone who tries to pull the wool over their eyes and hopes not to get found out.

When investors and lenders do their due diligence, they will find all the dirty laundry anyway. So, you might as well be up-front about it instead of risking them thinking you deliberately held back on important details which could have made a difference to their investment decisions.

You have nothing to gain from holding back, and everything to lose. This is not the time to make your business a hostage to your vanity.

Investors and lenders will understand. Professionals know the world isn't perfect. Only amateurs think that it is...or that it should be.

By being open, and demonstrating you have spotted your own problems, weaknesses, and blind spots, you show investors and lenders you are on track to get those problems sorted. Any lender or investor worth their salt will be fine with that.

In fact, here's another little-known secret.

Business plans which claim perfection can be a major red flag. They can lead to investors and lenders thinking they are either dealing with someone who either lacks the self-awareness to see where their gaps are or who isn't honest enough to own up to them. Or both.

So be positive. Be in sales mode. But be clear, open, and honest...even about the things that make you uncomfortable.

Any professional lender or investor worth dealing with will be fine. And if they're not, it's probably a major red flag for you that the investor or lender you're talking to might not be the right person to involve in your business going forward.

Keep it short

Finally, while this isn't a hard-and fast rule for every situation, try to keep the Executive Summary to a couple of pages if you can.

It's the headline, not the whole article.

It's the elevator pitch, not the whole sales presentation.

It's the appetiser, not the entrée.

You want to get the main points across, share your enthusiasm for your business and enthuse investors and lenders about its prospects for the future, while demonstrating you are worthy of their trust.

And then stop talking.

Professional investors will most likely head off to look at the Financial section next and they will review those numbers with whatever impression your Executive Summary left in their mind.

So make it good. Make it impactful. Make it enthusiastic.

Then let your numbers do the talking.

Executive Summary: Must-haves

- Mission statement
  Be clear what your business does, which markets you serve and how you serve them.

- Background
  Date of formation, legal structure, key staff, number of staff, physical locations, and any significant and events such as major industry awards or external accreditations.

- Financial performance
  Historic financial performance and future projections, in summary only. The detail should be kept for the Financial section later in the business plan. Use charts and graphs, if appropriate, to get key points across quickly, simply, and visually. You are creating a first impression here, not doing a line-by-line accounting analysis.

- <u>Start-ups</u>
  Rather than historic financial performance, set out the experience and background of your founders by highlighting their achievements and track records in previous roles.

  If you had a senior role at Google before setting up a new digital business or were previously a senior executive with a major player in the sector you intend to disrupt, sell investors and lenders hard on that in the absence of historic financial information.

- <u>Customers and markets served</u>
  What you sell and who you sell it to. If you sell a range of products, there is no need to list them all. Just give an idea of the major categories. "We sell replacement carburettors for major German automobile brands to the car enthusiast market" is all investors and lenders need to know at this stage. You will go into a lot more detail in the Products and Services section of your business plan.

- <u>Funding requirements</u>
  What funding are you looking for – debt, equity, a bit of both? Also set out any existing facilities with a brief note on utilisation over the past year or two to let potential investors and lenders see how much headroom you have in your current facilities and where any future pressures might arise.

- <u>Future plans</u>
  Make sure this excites investors and lenders – give them something to believe in and enthuse them with your dreams of a bright future (but be honest, rather than too starry-eyed)

- <u>And finally</u>
  Try to keep it to a couple of pages if you can.

Objective: Executive Summary

By the time investors and lenders have read your Executive Summary, they should be clear on the big picture for your business – where it has been, where it's headed and the great opportunities ahead…and, by extension, they should be clear that there are great opportunities for any investor or lender who comes on board at this stage.

Be passionate and enthusiastic, without going overboard, but make sure you can back up what everything you say in the sections to follow or you will be quickly found out.

Leave investor and lenders underwhelmed by your Executive Summary and it's an uphill struggle from here to stay out the "no" pile. They may not even read any further if they are not excited by your Executive Summary.

On the other hand, sell a convincing and exciting vision up-front and you will have investors and lenders rooting for you right out the starting gate, and in the right frame of mind to give you the support you need.

Company Overview: A strategic review

Although the Company Overview is the next section sequentially, remember professional investors and lenders are unlikely to read it immediately after the Executive Summary.

More likely they will check out the Financial section immediately after reading the Executive Summary. That's why it's worth investing the time you need to craft exceptional Executive Summary and Financial sections for your business plan.

If investors and lenders are still interested after reviewing those sections, they will come back to the Company Overview section to start filling in the details they need to make an investment decision.

And if they do that, your investors and lenders are already more than half-way sold.

Now you start to build on the emotional buy-in you secured in the Executive Summary by filling in the factual information investors and lenders need to corroborate their initial judgement that your business is one they want to back.

You can still lose them along the way from here, of course, especially if the excitement generated by the Executive Summary isn't sustained when investors and lenders dig deeper into the detail. But it's your game to lose from this point onwards.

Start by expanding on some of the facets of your business detail you mentioned briefly in the Executive Summary section, such as:

- The industry you're in – be as specific as you can. For example, it's not "manufacturing" or "automobile parts" but "replacement after-market carburettors for major German automotive brands".

- Your primary customer base – who do you sell to now, or intend to sell to in the future? Can you quantify metrics such as how many potential customers there are for your product or service, where they are in the world or the size of the market, in either physical units or monetary value terms (or ideally both)?

- The big problem you solve for customers. As the old saying goes, nobody **wants** a quarter-inch drill. What they really want is a quarter-inch hole. A quarter-inch drill is just one way to get that result. Talk about your customer needs in terms of quarter-inch holes, not quarter-inch drills.

- How you solve that big problem, at least in concept. You'll explain more about your products, services, and processes later in the document.

What is unique about this business?

Essentially, the company overview section explains why your business exists and the opportunities open to it.

Its purpose is to help investors and lenders understand the specific customer needs you serve in a well-defined market, and exactly how you meet them.

But you need to write it with the (often unspoken) question investors and lenders always have in mind when they look at a business plan, namely, "what is unique, special or different about this business compared to the rest of its sector?"

Professional investors and lenders know your business needs an edge of some sort to succeed in today's competitive markets. Understand what your edge is and how secure that position is will be an important part of their decision-making process.

For example, do you have intellectual property protection, like a trademark or a patent, or are there regulatory or financial barriers which make it difficult for new competitors to enter your market?

Being unique, special, or different can mean having a completely unique product or service for which you are the sole global provider, but that isn't always the case.

Many investors and lenders will support businesses which are not especially unique, especially if the business is a small one with modest funding needs.

However, the bigger the business, and the larger the amount of investment being sought, the more important it becomes that investors and lenders understand how your business is distinctively positioned within the markets it serves.

If that is not through a unique product or service, you might be able to demonstrate uniqueness in how you serve an existing need in a different way to the rest of your industry. That's fine too.

To give an example, although this is far from unique nowadays, a couple of decades ago you could serve almost any pre-existing market in a unique, new, highly cost-effective way just by getting your product manufactured in the Far East instead of in a major Western economy.

Going down that route could cut manufacturing cost for most businesses by half or more, while maintaining broadly comparable product quality.

Investors and lenders piled into opportunities to disrupt existing markets by developing that unique (at the time) approach to getting a whole range of relatively mundane products manufactured in a new, vastly cheaper way.

The products themselves were not unique, but the way they were manufactured and distributed at a dramatically lower price point was. That was the selling point for investors and lenders.

More recently, we have seen a similar dynamic as companies move their operations online instead of serving customers via traditional "bricks and mortar" outlets.

Again, the end-result isn't what makes those businesses unique.

The customer still ends up with a dress or a shirt or a mattress like they did before. But now they buy those items in a completely different way with an entirely different value proposition.

Both these trends are rather old hat now, but I include them for illustration purposes as some business owners struggle to explain what makes their business unique in their marketplace.

Developing a distinctive positioning for your business will serve you in so many ways in the future beyond just getting investors and lenders excited about your business plan.

Open your imagination and, if you don't think your business does anything especially unique now, think about how you can take the products and services you provide and re-cast them in a way which makes them stand out from your competition.

You don't need to keep going in the future the same way you've always done things in the past. You can change any time you like.

Developing your edge

I said earlier that one of the main reasons for preparing a business plan is because it benefits you and your business, whether you're looking for external funding or not.

Developing an edge, a unique and distinctive positioning for the products and services you sell, is a really good example how writing a business plan benefits you and your business even if you're not looking for external funding…and even if nobody outside your business ever reads your business plan.

Let's face it, if you can't explain what is unique about your products and services in a business plan, you're unlikely to be able to explain it to future potential customers either. That means your only option is slugging it out on price with the rest of the market to sign up customers, who in turn will desert you the minute someone else is a penny cheaper. That rarely ends well.

That's why it's worth doing a "dry run" of your distinctive positioning with investors and lenders.

If you think they are a tough bunch to persuade, just wait till you open the doors of your new venture and see how many customers walk into a business which doesn't give them a strong enough reason to patronise it over wherever they're buying from at the moment.

Any business without an edge of some sort is going to struggle in a competitive market. So, if you don't already have some degree of uniqueness or distinctiveness in what you do or how you do it, this might be a good time to develop that aspect of your business.

You don't need to discover a new vaccine, invent a new piece of technology, or have patents to cover what you do. But if your business is going to be successful, you need an edge over your competition in some shape or form, at least from the perspective of the niche segments of the market you sell to.

And, since you need to know what your edge is before targeting your chosen customers and creating your marketing campaigns, your business plan is a great place to work out all the wrinkles before you start spending big money with an advertising agency.

Of course, a good advertising agency can help polish your approach and present it in such a way as to really make it sing. But they can't invent something out of thin air. Your edge has got to be based on reality and that's the reality you will working out for yourself as you go through the process of creating your business plan.

Sometimes business owners struggle to think of ways they might be different from other businesses in their town or their sector, but this should never put you off. There are dozens...if not hundreds...of ways to provide a different way of doing things, even in highly competitive markets.

Questions to ask

If you are struggling with how to develop a distinctive positioning for your business here are some common ways that's done which might be worth considering:

- Who?
  Who do you serve - working moms...cycling enthusiasts...CEOs of Fortune 500 companies? As much as possible, clarify who your

ideal customer is. They may well have different needs to a mass-market solution, enabling you to tailor your product or service to make it highly attractive to specific customer groups.

- How?
  How do you serve them – by offering a superior product...better service...lower prices? What is it you do that other companies don't?

  Most businesses strive to undercut competitors' prices but that is by no means the only viable strategy, or even the most sensible one. Rolls Royce does well enough despite the fact you can buy a very decent car for a $1/10^{th}$ of the price of one of theirs.

- Method
  Maybe your uniqueness is not in the product itself – maybe it's because you manufacture it, ship it, or support it in ways that other providers don't. That can have benefits to customers which would make your product or service especially attractive.

  For example, lots of people buy shirts, but I'm pretty tall (6' 5") so I only buy from manufacturers whose shirts come with longer tails to make sure they don't get untucked when I sit down and stand up. To some extent, it's just a shirt, like dozens of manufacturers make. But for a tall person, the long tails make enough of a difference to change my purchasing decisions.

- Where?
  What about your location? If you are the only hairdresser in a town that isn't big enough to support two hairdressers, that's grounds for uniqueness.

Although, to flip that round, if a customer has to drive past a dozen of your competitors before getting to you, the likelihood is high that sooner or later they'll get out their cars a bit earlier. So, if you're not ultra-convenient you need to be doing something ultra-special to make sure your customers keep driving past all your competitors and come to you instead.

- Specializations
  Maybe your speciality is unique, even though the broad class of what you do isn't. Perhaps you run a law firm, but of the six law firms in your town, only yours specializes in employment law. Or you run the only hairdresser out of the six in your town to specialize in taking care of a bride's hair on her wedding day.

  Lawyers and hairdressers are not particularly unique, but in your area, those specializations underneath the broad banner of your profession might be.

- Service
  What about your service – do you offer 10-year guarantees when your competitors only offer 30-day guarantees...or next day delivery instead of 72-hour delivery...or 24/7 live customer service agents instead of a creaky website staffed by soulless automated customer service bots?

  Service is generally an easy way to differentiate, but that opportunity is rarely used to its fullest. Not only are you more likely to make a sale (at a similar price point, who wouldn't rather have a 10-year guarantee over a 30-day one?), even to non-customers you start building a reputation for quality and for standing behind your product which positions you favorably should they, or someone they know, need your product or service in the future.

Don't worry, you don't need to be unique in all these ways - that's probably an impossible dream anyway. But these are some of the common ways any business can create an edge over their competition, and they are all pretty easy to do once you put your mind to it.

Make sure you have something worth shouting about

If you are struggling to articulate how you demonstrate an edge in at least one of these areas (two or three is better), it might be worth getting back to the drawing board before you show your plan to a lender or investor.

When lenders or investors see a "same ol', same ol'" business plan in a highly competitive market with dozens of similar-looking, well-established competitors, the odds are high they won't take your proposal further.

A business without an edge is a hard business for investors and lenders to back.

However, even if they don't like your proposed edge, or don't think it's strong enough for them to fund your business, you still benefit from the feedback and perspective of a whole bunch of folk who aren't wrapped up in your business the way you, and the people who work for you, are.

If the overwhelming feedback from your potential sources of finance is that they don't feel your positioning is distinctive enough in your marketplace, that should tell you something.

More than likely, the people you are talking to as potential investors and lenders are not your target market for your products or services, but don't dismiss their comments out of hand "because they don't understand my market".

They probably don't.

But they do understand what a well-differentiated, well-positioned business looks like. And if you can't convince them you've got one of those, you're probably not going to convince your target customers either.

Don't let your ego get in the way. Accept the feedback and do something about it.

And if that isn't deciding to work harder to occupy a more unique position in your market and talk about it in a way which helps your customers better understand why they should deal with you instead of one of the other businesses in your sector, you've probably missed a golden opportunity.

Remember the outcome you want from a business plan isn't getting the funding you need.

The best outcome of all is developing a business model that really works, generating the profits and cash flow you need to reach your ambitions for your business.

Of course, securing additional funding can help make that happen. But funding alone won't turn a business that looks like every other business in its market, and lacks any unique positioning or differentiation, into a success.

For the Company Overview section, there is no need to set out a fully-fledged marketing proposal – that comes later.

But it is about highlighting the key ways your business stands out in the markets you serve.

The better you do that, the better your Company Overview section will be, and the more likely it is you will have created a better, more resilient business model in the process.

And, yes, it is also more likely, if you explain that well, you'll secure the funding you're looking for.

When you give investors and lenders a better understanding of the opportunities for your business, they start to understand how giving you the funding you need will generate attractive downstream returns for them.

If you can get investors and lenders as excited about that as you are, you have a winning proposal on your hands.

Company Overview: Must-haves

- Industry
  What industry are you in? Be as specific as possible. Not hairdressing, but bridal hair styling. Not a café, but a gourmet vegan café. Not motor parts, but after-market gearboxes for Japanese performance cars.

- <u>What?</u>
  What problem do you solve and how do you solve it? Talk more about your customer's quarter-inch hole problem than your quarter-inch drill solution.

- <u>Why?</u>
  Why is this a compelling problem for people to want to solve? Is there a significant downside to them continuing with how they do things now, or a considerable upside from your new, improved solution they wouldn't get from anywhere else?

- <u>Real world perspective</u>
  Make sure you have found a "real world" problem. The fact that something irritates you and you have found a way to fix it is great, but that doesn't mean there's a business in it.

- <u>Money</u>
  Even if you have discovered a real issue, and solved it, will people pay money for it? People endure all sorts of things because the problem doesn't feel like one they want to spend money putting right. As I heard someone put it once "just because there's a gap in the market, it doesn't mean there's a market in the gap".

  You are not just trying to solve problems. You are trying to solve problems people will pay money to fix. Otherwise, you have a hobby, not a business.

- <u>Your edge</u>
  What makes your business special. Be specific. None of this "we focus on quality" or "we put the customer first" stuff. Whether or not that's true, everyone says exactly the same thing, so investors

and lenders, along with real-world potential customers, just tune out expressions like those. All investors and lenders hear is "there is no compelling reason to buy from us, we're just like everyone else in our industry".

Be clear about how your business provides highly attractive alternatives to other solutions already available in the markets you serve.

And if you don't have an edge which stands up to external review, go and build one before you show your business plan to potential investors and lenders. "What is unique about your business in your target market?" is likely to be one of the first questions they ask.

Objective: Company Overview

When investors and lenders finish reading the Company Overview section, they should be clear on exactly what problem your business solves. Not what you sell, but what problem you solve.

Once you've done that, lead into an explanation about how your product or service solves that problem in a new or different way from other solutions on the market in at least some dimension.

Remember, however, it's not "different" customers care about. That's easy. There are hundreds of ways to be different.

For a successful business you need to be "better enough for customers to spend their hard-earned money with you".

Solving a problem in a way which is better enough for customers to choose your business over their current supplier is much tougher than just being different.

That's what investors and lenders are looking for. Your business plan should help them see that opportunity.

Market Analysis: Your business environment

The purpose of the Market Analysis section of your business plan is to demonstrate to investors and lenders you understand the market you operate in and the opportunities open to you.

Don't forget investors and lenders can also do this analysis for themselves and, for larger investments especially, they almost certainly will. So, your Market Analysis section needs to be firmly anchored in solid, reliable, verifiable data.

The last thing you want is for lenders or investors to do their own market analysis, only to find it some way adrift of what you claimed.

Potential investors and lenders would wonder whether you either hadn't done the analysis properly (leading to doubts about your competence) or whether you weren't being entirely honest with them (leading to doubts about your trustworthiness).

One way to minimise the chances of that happening – even by accident – is to use independent research and third-party sources to underpin the statements you make in this section.

That way investors and lenders don't just need to take you at your word. And even if their own research ultimately gives a slightly different answer, they won't think you were trying to trick them, just that your research sources had a different perspective from theirs.

The key here isn't just to repeat what you think is happening in your market. It's to demonstrate through evidence what's happening. More than occasionally, when business owners need to source evidence to back up what they say, what they thought the market was doing turns out to be very different from what it actually is doing.

Using external support

Although it's rarely necessary, drafting in some outside help to complete this section can seem like a tempting option to business owners who are not familiar with this style of evidence-based research.

One word of warning, though – if you decide to draft somebody in to do the research for you, be careful to choose someone who is clearly highly independent from you and your business, with no axe to grind one way or the other. If you don't, you're almost certainly wasting your money.

Investors and lenders aren't stupid.

They know if you engage some random consultant, especially one without a "knocking it out the park" level of specialist knowledge and insight, there is at least a possibility they have some undisclosed relationship with you which could compromise their objectivity and may lead to a less rigorous approach than investors and lenders would normally look for.

Don't set yourself a mountain to climb by having to restore credibility you didn't need to lose in the first place. Either choose someone who is clearly extremely independent or don't bother and just do it yourself, would be my advice.

Sources of research which investors and lenders would generally consider suitably independent include:

- Research done by someone with an appropriate professional accreditation, eg a CPA, for whom there are personal and professional sanctions if they mess things up. They're generally seen as a reliable source of research because they've got too much to lose personally from being anything other than objective.

- Universities. Investors and lenders tend to believe that Professor So-and-So who is an expert in a relevant field will have used all their PhD-powered ninja research tricks to carry out a competent piece of research they can rely on.

- Your local government economic development arm. In their case, the research you need might already exist – just ask and they will tell you. As a bonus, you should normally be able to present their findings as part of your report without charge as most government reports are public domain documents and therefore freely available.

- Trade bodies. They often publish reports on the markets you serve and economic developments affecting your sector – the number of people buying their first house or the amount an average household spends on pet food, for example. Sometimes you need to pay for these insider reports, but they usually have data you couldn't get elsewhere without considerable expense, so they can be great value.

If none of those work for you, think very carefully before you spend a lot of money on this part of your business plan.

Plenty of people will be happy to help and charge you for the privilege, but if the source isn't one that your lenders or investors will see as at least reasonably objective you are probably wasting your money.

The only exception to this general rule, if you already have a good idea of who your preferred lender or investor would be, is to ask them to recommend someone to do the research for this part of the business plan on your behalf.

By definition, they will trust whoever they recommend, so your job of providing information which your lenders or investors will be prepared to rely on is already 90% or more of the way there.

And if you do end up doing this yourself, don't worry. That's what many business owners do. And it's not as difficult as you might think.

The do-it-yourself option

If you end up completing this section without external support, all you need to do is instil confidence in the claims you make in your business plan. And you do that by giving the details of where you got your information from as you're going along.

If you say there are 100,000 people in your town, for example, demonstrate that number has been drawn from the most recent local census.

That information will be publicly available. Just cite the source and include a hyperlink in a footnote to demonstrate to investors and lenders that this is a genuine number. Do that, and nobody will question your claim that 100,000 people live in your town.

If you say there are six other hairdressers in town, include a screenshot of the Google search you did on a particular date to let potential lenders or investors see the evidence with their own eyes.

If you say your competitors charge $X for their almost identical product, include a copy of the pages from their catalogue or a link to the online store on their website.

If you say you supply services to a $100 million market, include a copy of the report from a relevant trade body which demonstrates that is the size of the market.

The basic principle is this – every time you state a fact or make a claim you should state where you got that information from, and the source should be as objective and independently verifiable as possible.

Investors and lenders are unlikely to check each one, but if they check a handful of the stats in your business plan to verifiable third-party sources and your claims check out, that's a big confidence boost.

The issues you might want to explore in the Market Analysis section of your business plan to ensure investors and lenders have all the information they need to make an investment decision include:

- The current size of the industry, ideally in both physical units and monetary value.

- How much has the industry has grown in the past and what rate of future growth is projected?

- What trends are occurring in your industry and how do they affect businesses in your sector. Is it a growing market or a declining market, and if so, at what rate?

- Within the broad industry you serve, which customers do you intend to target? What are their specific needs and how do they currently try to address those needs?

- The demographic and socioeconomic information which underpins your target market (age, gender, income, employment status and so on).

- The size of your target market, within the broader industry you serve. How much do customers in the particular niche you target spend each year on products and services like yours? How often do they purchase...once a year, once a week, daily? Are their purchases completely seasonal, like Christmas trees, a weekend treat, or an everyday purchase?

- How is the market carved up between existing suppliers now, and what percentage of your target market can you reasonably expect to acquire? Be realistic – if there are six hairdressers in town but for your business plan to work, you need to be doing 80% of your town's hairstyling from a standing start, investors will know that is unlikely to happen.

- In what ways might competitors find it difficult to enter your target market, eg a high level of initial investment, an offputtingly strict regulatory regime, or problems finding enough qualified staff to support their business as it grows?

- Who are your major competitors? How do you compare against them in each of the categories above, for example your growth rate vs theirs, or the different market niches you each serve – one might concentrate on younger people and another on an older demographic, for example.

- What are your competitors' key strengths and weaknesses? In what ways might they make it difficult for you to succeed?

This section will take a significant amount of research, but it's time well spent.

First and foremost, it prepares you to succeed – and don't forget, the main reason you write a business plan is not to produce a sterile, theoretical document for investors and lenders.

Its primary purpose is to benefit you and your business by giving you a clear idea for where you're headed and a compelling vision for how you're going to get there.

Secondly, it helps investors appreciate you have done all the homework they can reasonably expect, and the claims you make are backed up with external evidence where possible which helps demonstrate they can trust you.

That is essential because no-one in their right mind will invest in or lend money to a business owner they don't trust. Time and effort spent on this section will always be time and effort well spent.

Market Analysis: Must-haves

- Market size
  The current size of your target market, with historic growth rates and future projections, based ideally on independent third-party reports or research.

- Market trends
  The trends are affecting your sector, whether that's the result of steady, long-term change or impending technical developments which could transform your market in the years to come.

- Target customers
  Within the broad industrial category you operate in, which customers specifically are you targeting, and how do their needs differ from the rest of the sector? Where – if anywhere – do they buy from now and what are the strengths and weaknesses of their current supplier?

- Demographic information
  Describe the demographic and socioeconomic makeup of your target customer base (age, gender, income, employment status, and so on), including a comparison with key competitors where relevant.

- Purchasing habits
  How much do your target customers spend now on products and services like yours? Provide a breakdown of any relevant purchasing habits, eg seasonality, purchase frequency, price-consciousness.

- Target market share
  What percentage of your target market can you reasonably expect to acquire and over what timescale? Make sure this is a realistic assessment of both the ultimate market share you are seeking to build and the timescales over which you expect to make that happen.

- Barriers to entry
  Outline the difficulties any competitors might experience trying to enter your target market, such as regulatory, financial, or operational challenges.

- Competitor analysis
  Who are your major competitors and how do you compare against them in some of the key metrics above. What market share do they have and is it growing or shrinking? What are their key strengths and weaknesses?

Objective: Market Analysis

In your Market Analysis section, you need to help investors and lenders understand the market you operate within and how you fit into it, relative to your main competitors.

This isn't just a matter of intellectual curiosity. Investors and lenders are trying to understand if the potential market for your products and services is both big enough, and open enough to your offer, to give your business a reasonable chance of reaching its revenue targets in the timescale you set.

Investors and lenders also want to have a weather-eye out for anything that could get in the way of your plans, such as a slew of well-funded, well-entrenched competitors.

The Market Analysis section also lays some of the groundwork you will come back to in your marketing plan.

Clearly your marketing strategy will be entirely different if you are one of hundreds of small businesses slugging it out for the same customers, compared to a start-up trying to get traction against two huge competitors. The Market Analysis section is where you start to set that context for investors and lenders.

Investors and lenders want to be reassured that your marketing strategy seems plausible given the structure of the market you operate in. So, make sure your Market Analysis and Sales and Marketing sections cross-reference one another and clearly demonstrate they are both part of one cohesive plan (sadly, this is not as common as you might imagine).

Organization and Management: How it all works

The Organization and Management section of your business plan is where you show investors and lenders how your business is organized and structured and how it operates on a day-to-day basis.

You also start to lay out some elements of your cost structure in this section, particularly your staffing costs which are one of the two or three biggest expense categories in nearly every business.

Legal structure

Before we get into the detail of your staffing costs, it is best to start by laying out the legal and regulatory environment your business operates within. Make sure you cover topics such as:

- The legal form it operates under.

- Why you chose that option if the reason isn't immediately obvious.

- The stakeholders you deal with, including existing investors and major providers of finance.

- The government bodies or regulatory authorities under whose licences or oversight your business is required to operate.

- Any overseas regulatory bodies or governmental relationships which are key to the success of your business.

- Licensing arrangements which are significant to your business, such as import and export licenses or licenses to use intellectual property such as patents, trademarks, or branding.

Staffing structure

Once you have mapped out the legal and regulatory environment for your investors and lenders, start breaking out the internal operational structure of your business.

Here you show how your business works "under the hood", split into its various internal components – the different teams, departments and sections within your business, the range of locations you operate from, and the key personnel you rely on to achieve your business objectives.

There are no hard-and-fast rules for how any business should be structured, so don't feel you have to structure your business in some "conventional" way if that isn't how you actually operate in practice. After all, that might be part of what gives your business the edge we spoke about earlier.

However, the way you explain your operating environment in this section should mirror the way you run your business in practice otherwise it gets very confusing to report to investors and lenders about your business on a different basis than you operate it in practice.

That said, the most common ways businesses tend to organise themselves is around product lines, geography or industries served.

To give some examples, if your business is primarily organised around the different product lines you sell, use that structure to explain "we have 75 people working on Product A, 59 people working on Product B", and so on.

If your business is structured according to geography, you might say "in our New England division we have 35 people, in the Mid-West 49", and so on.

Equally, if you have one team serving the major global automotive manufacturers while another serves after-market repair shops, use that structure to explain how your business is organised.

You might also add in a section about what functions operate from Head Office, if you have one, as opposed to what activities take place out in the operating divisions.

Maybe all your Legal, Finance and Marketing runs from Head Office, with people from there going to local offices to attend to local needs as required. Alternatively, every local office might have a mini-head office team to pick up issues on the ground without needing people to travel across the country to sort out minor local HR or marketing issues.

No matter how your business is structured, though, an organization chart is always helpful.

If you employ more than 20 people or so don't worry about naming every single individual on it.

Investors and lenders don't need to know everyone's name. They just want an idea of how many people work in each department as an indication of the scale of your operation.

A structure to departmental level with a named manager and a box underneath saying something like "35 electrical engineers" or "14 warehouse operatives" is perfectly acceptable.

Knowing the structure, the fact that a suitably qualified and experienced manager is in place and having some idea of the depth of expertise in key areas of your business is what investors and lenders are looking for.

They are not looking to understand how your workforce operates in minute detail. They just want to understand how your business is organised and how your cost base knits together.

Financial implications

Investors and lenders are always keen to understand where the costs are in your business, which departments are the most expensive to operate, whether the balance of cost is right across departments, and so on.

They will pick out anomalies and ask questions if, for example, your 20-person business has three people in its HR Department (not saying that proportion would never be right, just that it would be an unusual balance which needs explaining).

However, investors and lenders are primarily interested in understanding how your chosen organizational structure, whatever that may be, impacts the major elements of cost in your business. Often, in large part, that is driven by your organisation structure and the salaries and benefits which flow from that structure.

For example, investors and lenders are not terribly bothered that Jane in accounts earns $45,372 a year. But they would be extremely interested to learn that the $1million a year you spend on engineering staff is 60% of your total salary and benefits budget.

So make sure that information is readily available and explained, especially when that might look unusual to an outside observer – why you employ truck drivers directly rather than outsourcing to one of the major trucking firms, for example.

Again, that is not because it's never right to hire your own truck drivers, web developers, social media team or any other function that can be, and often is, outsourced. It might be entirely the right decision to keep that resource in-house for your business.

Just explain it. And in specific, quantifiable ways, not just "we like to be in control" or "the quality is higher".

While both those statements might be true, an experienced investor who has seen other proposals from within your industry will pick up on staffing costs which appear out of line.

Not only is the level of cost important when it comes to staffing expenses, but so is the type of cost.

Are your staffing expenses mainly fixed costs (such as if most of your staff are on fixed monthly salaries) or variable costs (that is, costs move up and down depending a trackable metric such as the number of hours worked, units produced, or a predetermined share of that month's profits)? Or perhaps a bit of both?

As a general rule, internal costs represent a regular monthly commitment and outside service providers, like trucking companies, tend to be paid on a unit basis, eg by the package delivered, hour worked, etc.

When times are hard, having a large portion of your cost base as a fixed monthly commitment increases the risks for investors and lenders, so they like to have a good handle on how flexible your model is in the face of fluctuations in customer demand, both up and down.

The 1-2-3 Method revisited

This might be a good time to revisit the 1-2-3 Method we spoke about earlier as staff costs can often be a significant issue when fluctuations in business activity, both up and down, hit your business.

Help investors and lenders understand how flexible your staffing costs are in the event of changes in customer demand. What would happen if your sales revenues went up by 20%? Or down by a similar number?

Are you stuck with an inflexible cost base where everyone gets a straight monthly salary? Or do you run your business with a core full-time team, supplemented by freelancers and contractors to cater for peaks and troughs in activity?

Either is fine, and both have advantages and disadvantages. Don't believe anyone who tells you that logistics should always be outsourced, or marketing should always be in-house. Any option can work, it just depends which option works best in the specific context of your business.

Just explain what you do and why. That helps investors and lenders understand how your cost base works, when it comes to staff costs, and what degree of flex is built in to cater for significant changes in customer demand.

If you make more than occasional use of freelancers and contractors, be sure to include them within the relevant department on your organization chart and color-code or highlight them in some way to indicate their employment status.

Your Marketing Department, for example, might have a core team of six people on a salary, but at busy times of the year they might be supplemented by another six people on a freelance or contractor basis who, on average, work half the year each.

In that situation, your organization chart should show the six full-time people on salaries alongside the cost of those people and, separately analysed, the equivalent of a further three full time staff working under contracts (six people for half the year each, on average) together with the costs associated with them.

By presenting your staff costs this way, investors and lenders can see how your organisation structure and your cost structure fit together in the context of the overall objectives you set out earlier in your business plan.

It also gives them the clarity they look for over what is almost certain to be a major monthly expense item for your business.

Organization and Management: Must-haves

- Legal structure
  Is your business an S-Corp, C-Corp, partnership, sole trader, etc?

- Ownership
  Who owns the stock? Are there any complex features such as multiple classes of stock with different voting rights or performance-related options coming due, which could dilute the interest of any incoming investor?

  If you operate as a partnership, outline the share of profits each partner is entitled to and any significant capital contributions each partner has made.

- Your team
  The background and experience of key members of your team. Investors want to know you have the team of experienced, successful, well-qualified individuals you need to deliver your business plan

  A brief paragraph or two is plenty at this point. You can include more detailed resumes in the appendices if you want. Just point investors and lenders to where they can find those later in your business plan document.

- Unusual circumstances
  Any highly specific staffing dependencies and agreements – for example, the five-year consultancy contract with the MIT professor who developed your product or the senior salesperson who gets a percentage off the top for everything they bring in.

  Anything beyond a straight salary or normal freelancer/contractor arrangement should be explained here if it represents a significant cost to your business. It's not that it's wrong, or that lenders or investors will want to unpick what's already in place (at least, not as a rule). But they need to understand how your cost base knits together, so if there are any unusual arrangements in your business, be sure to describe them here.

- Labor market dynamics
  Especially for in-demand skills in your local area, if you can't attract enough suitably qualified staff, that's likely to be a bigger

obstacle to the long-term success of your business than the lack of finance. It is a lot easier to find a source of finance than it is to find highly in-demand skills, especially if you are setting up a new business without an established track record.

Investors and lenders know from experience that skill shortages tend to result in above-average pay rises until the business is paying enough to attract the right calibre of, and number of, people. They will want to be assured that your business plan is realistic and reflects the market for the skills you need in your local area.

- Skills gaps
  Describe any current-day gaps in your organization structure which need addressing and any key hires you will need in the future as your business grows.

  Perhaps you plan to hire another marketing person in a year's time to support further expansion, or you intend to open up a new office in an area you don't currently serve. These are positive signs for investors and lenders, but make sure you put the people you will need in the future into your business plan to demonstrate you are thinking ahead.

- An organisation chart
  Show key departments, your management structure, and the personnel in each department (individually if you run a small business, but just the number of people in each department if you employ more than 20/25 people).

- Staffing costs
  Either within the organisation chart or separately, show the staff cost for each department including benefits and payroll taxes as well as base salaries.

  If you make significant use of freelancers or contractors as part of your operations, itemise them separately and highlight their costs within the overall departmental costs.

Objective: Organization and Management

In this section you are trying to do three things.

Firstly, you're showing investors and lenders that you have an appropriate legal and regulatory structure to deliver your business objectives.

Secondly, you're demonstrating you have the team you need to make those objectives happen (or a plan to get them before you need them).

Finally, you're introducing some outline information about your people costs which will flow through into the Financial section later in your business plan.

This gives investors and lenders context around the size and scale of your business and helps them understand the operational reasons behind any apparent anomalies, which means they will be less inclined to challenge those when they come to the Financial section of your plan.

Products and Services: Why they matter

We introduced your products and services earlier in your business plan when we talked about identifying the needs of your customers and demonstrating how you meet those needs in as distinctive a way as possible in the markets you serve.

The Products and Services section is where we need to add the next level of detail.

You might think this section comes a little late in the business plan as most business owners obsess over their products and services first and foremost...as they should, of course.

However, investors and lenders have entirely different criteria to business owners.

Fundamentally, investors and lenders want to be as comfortable as possible that the dividends or interest payments due to them will be paid on time and, at some date in the future, they will get their money back.

And who can blame them? We would want exactly the same if we invested our own money in a business where we didn't have day-to-day control.

Another reason the specifics of your products and services do not appear quite so prominently in the sights of investors and lenders is that they will usually be investing across a range of sectors.

A local bank, for example, will look after hundreds of small business clients. They can't possibly hope to understand every detail of every product and service across the dozens of sectors their customers operate in.

While the product is usually the most important thing to a business owner, investors and lenders know they will never know as much about that as the business owner and, frankly, usually don't even try.

Of course, investors and lenders realise your products and services are what will ultimately make your business successful.

They just happen to be the elements of your business in which investors and lenders probably have the least amount of technical expertise...and certainly a good deal less knowledge than someone who has worked in the sector for many years.

So, for investors and lenders, the first stage of the decision-making process is usually to see whether the aspects they do understand, such as the financial returns, the marketing strategy and the company's growth trajectory make it an investment they want to get involved with.

Only when there are green lights against all of those will investors and lenders start digging into the product itself. They can always bring in an expert of their own later if they need a deeper technical understanding in the specifics of your product or service.

Pitching to a non-expert

Although you will be steeped in the lore of your business and the wider industry it operates within, it is worth remembering the first person who reads your business plan will almost certainly not be an expert in your product or sector.

Especially in larger firms, a non-expert gatekeeper or junior staff member might be tasked with reviewing all the business plans received and doing some "rough cuts", such as turning down proposals from sectors which investors or lenders have decided not to invest in for whatever reason, and some elementary analysis to identify how attractive your business is as a funding prospect.

For smaller amounts of funding, the likelihood is that a specialist will never examine the technicalities of your product and service in full.

For larger amounts of funding the stakes are much higher, so it is more likely that prospective investors or lenders will get either an in-house specialist of their own or an external third party to review the technical aspects of your business to help them understand how large a market opportunity your product or service represents.

If your proposal goes that far, the technical experts will clearly need a level of detail about your product or service and how it works that goes beyond the knowledge base of a casual reader.

But you have to get your proposal past an initial non-expert reviewer first and get them excited about the opportunities in your business plan. So, as much as possible, avoid using industry jargon or buzzwords since your initial audience is unlikely to have a full technical appreciation of what they mean.

You can always put a full technical spec in the appendices if you feel a technical reviewer would benefit from a deeper level of insight than you would want to include in a section designed primarily with a non-technical reviewer in mind.

Concentrate on helping a non-industry expert see what you see, understand the opportunity you spotted, and grasp how your plan is perfectly positioned to take advantage of a market which is desperate for the products or services your business provides.

You have to get over that hurdle before you need to worry too much about the finer technical specifications for your product or service that only someone with a similar technical background to yours could fully appreciate and understand.

The importance of objectivity

For most business owners, the most challenging part of this section is not getting themselves stoked up enough to demonstrate a high level of enthusiasm for their product or service. Usually that comes naturally to business owners talking about their own products and services.

The tricky bit is getting the objectivity you need to explain your products or services to a third party from first principles. That is much harder than it sounds.

Business owners have often spent years developing their own product or service. So much so, they fell in love with it quite some time ago. Ever since then, their ability to be completely rational about it has gradually faded away as the years passed.

They are committed to their product or service and want to make it a success, which is great. But sometimes it's clear they have lost the perspective they need to be completely objective about their products and services.

Every time Gordon Ramsay turns up at a failing restaurant for his Kitchen Nightmares series, he finds a wildly enthusiastic business owner who is 100% convinced they serve the best food in town, but for some reason they don't understand, the restaurant has no customers.

The restaurant owner sees 90% of their customers not coming back after a single meal at their restaurant and concludes their customers don't have as finely-developed a palate as theirs, rather than seeing the situation for what it is – their food is terrible.

The restaurant owner's passion (however misplaced) tends to have remained undimmed throughout, but their lack of objectivity ultimately landed them in hot water. It's not passion they're lacking. It's objectivity.

Once that objectivity has been restored, courtesy of Chef Ramsay, the business gets back on track and quickly recovers the clientele it lost.

That's why the Products and Services section of your business plan can be challenging for business owners to complete.

For perhaps the first time in years, business owners need to try and see their business as others might see it, because that's the perspective investors and lenders...and indeed future potential customers...will be coming from.

If a typical customer buys from you once and never comes back, it will be obvious to investors and lenders that this business has some pretty significant issues which the owner doesn't seem willing to address.

Your investors and lenders don't even need to understand why, or even whether, objectively, you or your customers are right in their assessment. Any business without customers is not going to last long, and no investor or lender wants to be the "good money after bad" slice of the financial pie.

And remember, if you can't talk about your products and services in ways which are compelling enough to get prospective investors and lenders excited, the chances of you being able to get real, live customers excited about your products and services once you go to market is not very high either.

If lenders or investors have read this far in your business plan, it means they like what they have seen up till now. They bought into your dream. They just need to understand enough of the detail behind your products and services to translate that dream into reality in their minds.

The way you do that is by helping investors and lenders see this isn't some pie-in-the-sky project that works fine in theory but would never work in the real world, or where you have an unrealistic or over-optimistic view of the market's appetite for your products and services.

Demonstrate objectivity about your products and services, and their future prospects, and you'll carry investors and lenders over the "credibility line" and put them firmly in your corner, ready to argue your case inside their organization.

Time to get into the details

So how do you get investors and lenders excited about your business plan?

I'm sorry to say, unless you're a celebrity, however strong you think your personal brand or reputation is, it probably won't be enough to get lenders or investors excited about a me-too product or service.

If you're a former professional sports star opening up a bar in the town where you had your best years as a player, like Sam Malone in "Cheers", that celebrity cachet might be enough. But those situations are rare, so you might be better off working on the assumption that you need an approach that does not rely on your fame, notoriety, or networks to drum up trade.

Apart from anything else, for your business to have long-term value, it can't be all about your personal brand otherwise you can never step away from it.

All the value in Sam Malone's bar was tied up with his role in it – without that, "Cheers" would be just another basement bar, worth a fraction of what it used to be when Sam served the drinks there.

To be assured of some longevity, beyond you, in the business, investors and lenders are looking to understand what you sell, not who's selling it, in the Products and Services section.

How, specifically, does it work…how do the components come together…what is the manufacturing process…what expertise do you need…what intellectual property protection do you have…that's the sort of information investors and lenders are looking for.

They also want to understand, in more depth than you have explained previously, exactly how your product and service is better than your competition.

Earlier in your business plan you might well have said something like your product lasts twice as long as everyone else's or sells for half the price.

For getting the concept across in the early sections of your business plan, that level of understanding is enough to get investors and lenders thinking in the right direction.

Now is the time to back up those claims with evidence.

If your product lasts twice as long, what are you doing differently to everyone else on the market that makes it more durable – do you, for example, use different materials, employ a different manufacturing process, or provide extended care and maintenance services to extend the life of your product?

If you can afford to sell it for half the price and still make a reasonable profit, what are you doing differently from the rest of the sector – have you, for example, developed a completely new manufacturing process, or sourced materials from a different provider with a markedly lower cost base, or developed a new way to assemble your product which dramatically lowers factory labor costs relative to your competitors?

As you go through the Products and Services section, bear in mind this is the section investors and lenders will be the most sceptical about.

Partly because this is the section they are likely to understand the least from a technical perspective, so you will need to convince them from first principles that your proposal is credible and reliable.

But mostly it's because every investor and lender has seen hundreds of "miracle products" over the years that nobody bought and just as many "innovative services" that nobody cared about.

Anyone who invests in or lends to your business is ultimately concerned about getting their money back, and professional investors and lenders know that, without an excellent product for which there is strong customer demand, getting their money back is going to be unlikely...hence their interest in this section and the degree of scepticism they feel (whether or not they admit to it outright).

Credibility counts

Building credibility in the products and services you sell is absolutely key in this section of your business plan because that's where the biggest risks are from an investor or lender's perspective.

If your first marketing campaign doesn't work, there's plenty of time to develop another one without troubling the financial stability of your business too much. But if your product or service turns out to be a dud, there are not many ways back from that. And, certainly, no inexpensive ones.

While I encourage business owners to be more sales-orientated in their business plan than they usually are instinctively, the Products and Services section is one area you want to dial that right back.

Take the time to explain exactly how your product or service works and why the features you are building in make it better, in some material way, than whatever your competitors do now.

If what you sell has a technology, scientific or engineering component to it, make sure you include conceptual diagrams, an explanation of the technology and how it works, details of how you ensure the quality of the end-product, any specific variations you need to allow for – local regulations might mean technical standards are different in the European market than in the US, for example.

If part of what you do is covered by a patented process or some other intellectual property rights, make sure you explain what protections you have and how that impacts on your end-product.

However you describe your products or services, be positive, of course, but be measured and factual with it.

You need to convince investors and lenders that your product or service works as well as you claim it does.

That it's good enough to occupy a commanding position in the markets you serve.

That it's reliable enough to compete with existing solutions.

That all the potential wrinkles in design and production have been thought through.

That your lab tests and market tests have been conducted in a suitably independent scientific manner and have been constructed in such a way as to present meaningful statistical results.

The list goes on and on.

But hopefully the message is clear. In the Products and Services section, you need to go overboard on establishing the credibility of what you sell. If the credibility scale normally goes up to 10, you want to get it up to 11 when investors and lenders read your business plan.

You will only do that if you put your own preconceptions and your own understandable love for what you do on one side and approach this section of your business plan with the mindset of someone who has never heard of your business, your products or your services before this moment.

Because, odds are, that is exactly the frame of mind the person who picks up your business plan document for the first time at a bank or investment house will have.

They will probably know very little about your business and your sector and they will be sceptical of outlandish claims about transforming the world unless you can back that up with cold, hard evidence, linked back to a compelling story of the future opportunities for your business.

They won't be against you as a matter of principle, but you need to get them on your side from a position of, at least, neutral scepticism, by establishing as much credibility as you can muster when it comes to demonstrating your products and services live up to your claims.

Your product or service should really shine through in this section. It should be abundantly clear both to investors and lenders that you have something unique to offer and you are in a prime position to attract customers who are desperate to fill needs which are not being met at the moment by their current supplier.

Security of supply

This particularly applies for businesses selling physical products, but it can be an issue for service-based businesses too.

At the moment I'm doing some work for a professional service firm with a national reputation in a very niche part of their field. One of their biggest headaches is finding suitably qualified and experienced staff to do the skilled professional work their clients require. While their profession at a headline level is not that unusual, people with the niche expertise they need are few and far between.

Similarly, if you want to hire computer programmers in Silicon Valley or top-grade investment bankers on Wall Street in order to have the human resources necessary to service your client needs, the right people for your business are not exactly ten-a-penny.

In the same way as a producer of physical products would be impacted by a strike at a component supplier, say, a provider of services won't have any revenues to bill if they can't find enough people with the relevant skills, qualifications and expertise to do the work clients have briefed them to carry out.

Sometimes the availability of skilled people in the service sector can be as much of a "security of supply" issue as key materials or components would be for a seller of physical products.

Either way, you need to be explicit about where the bottlenecks are in your operation and how you will ensure the right quantities at the right quality will be on-hand at the right time to meet customer demand.

Are you dependent on smoothly functioning international supply chains, for example?

Perhaps the cost of a key component is determined by the prices on volatile international commodity markets – if so, you need to decide how you would manage the financial risk of significant price fluctuations.

Or maybe there are only one or two global producers for a key element of your product, meaning you might be exposed to fluctuations in both cost and supply.

You also need a plan for how to handle trade embargos, dock strikes, boats sinking in storms and some of the other less-than-predictable aspects of international logistics.

Whether you sell physical products or services, investors and lenders will want to understand the degree of control you have over all the key elements you need to make and sell your product or service.

They will understand that it is not always possible to have complete control over everything you would ideally like to control, but where your control is limited, you need to explain what you are doing to mitigate any risks and ensure your business won't come to a halt due to key materials not being available or commodity price hikes making your business uneconomic.

Product profitability

Finally, in this section, break down the costs of the product, or products if you have more than one, to help investors and lenders understand how your costing structure works.

Ideally you should separate out both the added value on your product and the gross margin.

Added value is the selling price of your product less the materials you need to buy in to make it – the sheets of aluminium, the sub-assemblies, and the glass windows if you're an automobile manufacturer, for example. If you run a service business you might have few or none of these, but if you sell a physical product you definitely will.

Your gross margin is the added value after deducting what are called "direct costs". These include the employment costs for the people who directly produce what you sell and any other direct costs of production...which broadly means any elements without which you couldn't produce your finished product.

The definition of this is a very literal one. You would not be able to produce a finished product for long without oil to lubricate the machines you use to make it, for example. But you could produce your finished product without a single member of your management team.

Although this is slightly more controversial, I often get my professional services clients to think of costs like professional indemnity insurance and professional body memberships as a direct cost. That's because they can't practice, and therefore bill clients, unless they're a member of a relevant professional body and are covered by a mandated amount of professional indemnity insurance.

As they are not permitted to work for clients without those in place, I encourage them to think about those costs as direct costs of production rather than overhead costs which is how most businesses account for insurance-type costs.

By thinking of their cost base in this way, it helps business leaders understand their cost structure better and makes the drivers of their costs clearer.

This might be better explained by a simple example.

If a law firm takes out half of its fee-earning staff, by and large their professional indemnity insurance charges would reduce by half too. Whereas building insurance costs for their office would remain constant, regardless of how many people worked in there.

That makes, in a way that I accept accounting purists might disagree with, the cost of professional indemnity insurance more like a direct cost than an overhead cost, such as building insurance.

This precise example might not apply to you if you don't run a law firm, but I find many service businesses have more direct costs (in the sense that, without them, they couldn't provide the service) than they think they do, and an apparently high level of overhead costs sometimes just means a potential misunderstanding of how the cost drivers in their business really work.

Whether you run a product-based business or a service-based business it is immensely helpful to have a thorough understanding of how your cost base is built up and what the main drivers are for each cost heading. That way, you are more likely to make better financial decisions.

And, of course, it also has the benefit of helping your investors and investors understand how your business finances work than they would do otherwise.

At this point in your business plan, don't go any deeper into cost base analysis than this. There will be more details of your running costs and overheads in the Financial section. In the Products and Services section your focus should be entirely on the economics of your product or service.

Sometimes a diagram can be helpful.

I have seen the cost breakdown for a bakery using slices of a cake as a metaphor – a quarter of the cake is raw materials like flour, butter and eggs, another 40% is salaries for the workers in the bakery, and so on. That worked well.

I have also seen the cost structure for a coffee shop shown as marks on the side of a coffee mug – a tiny slice at the bottom was the cost of coffee itself, then a bit more was the milk and sugar, a bit more still was the baristas' salaries, and so on.

Similarly, a construction company's cost base could be portrayed as the floors on a high-rise building.

You get the idea. Sometimes a picture or a diagram make it easier to get your point across in a way that investors and lenders instantly understand. If there is a way of doing that which links back to the products and services your business sells, without over-doing the metaphor, then it can be an excellent way to explain your business to investors and lenders.

Products and Services: Must-haves

- <u>Fill in the details</u>
  Building on the product or service information you gave in the

Company Overview section, look to build a deeper understanding from there as investors and lenders should now have that high-level conceptual approach (faster, cheaper, longer lasting, etc) model fixed in their minds.

- Non-technical language
Remember a first stage review may not be done by a subject matter expert. Don't patronise the front-line people you meet at banks or investment houses as they'll be smart people who have seen a lot more business plans than you probably have.

But explain everything in terms any reasonably smart non-technical person can understand, without dumbing down the facets that make your product or service particularly attractive to the markets you serve.

- The detail behind your points of difference
Highlight why your product is different from other potential solutions already in the market, and why that makes it more attractive to customers.

Without getting into the marketing of it (which is our next section) you need to get across that, for example, your solution is 30% cheaper because you use different materials, or that it eliminates a historic weak point in the manufacturing process, so lasts twice as long as your competitors' products.

- Credibility
You need to make sure this section of your business plan is very measured, evidence-based, and well-researched. It is the one element investors and lenders probably are less likely to fully

understand, especially if you sell a highly technical product or service, and it's therefore the area of your business plan they'll most need to be convinced is realistic.

So you need to convince them you have a solid, reliable product which delivers on the promises you make to your target customers – improved service, cost savings, additional features, or whatever your promise might be.

- This is not your marketing plan
  Don't get too hung up on USPs and marketing jargon at this point – and, ideally, avoid jargon of all sorts in this section if you can.

  Investors and lenders want to understand the differences between your product or service and the others on the market, together with the broad tack you intend to take when selling to potential customers (eg is it a higher-quality product, cheaper than existing providers or a completely innovative solution to a common problem). They don't need a fully worked-up marketing plan – not in this section at least.

- Intellectual property
  If your product or service depends on intellectual property protection, be very clear about what protection you have – patents granted, trademarks registered, and the like.

  And be clear about who owns that intellectual property – do you own it personally, does your business own it and pay you a royalty, does a third party own it and you pay them a licence fee? This is a very important consideration for any potential lender or investor.

- Sensitivities
  What sensitivities might affect your ability to run your business –
  where might labor disputes, an extended supply chain,
  international trade embargos or a limited number of potential
  suppliers create issues, and what plans do you have to manage
  those scenarios should they arise.

- Security of supply
  Are there any risks to your ability to secure the supplies you need
  at a fair price? And if so, what are you doing to offset at least
  some of that risk?

  Maybe you keep a "safety stock" of key items on-site to make
  sure short-term supply chain issues won't impact your business
  significantly, perhaps you hedge your commodity prices in the
  financial markets to minimise the impact of short-term price
  fluctuations, perhaps you retain a roster of suppliers so if one
  goes out of business you can get what you need from another
  one.

- Finalizing your product
  If you don't have a finished product or service yet, map out the
  steps you're taking to finalize it. Specifically, spell out the research
  and development actions you are taking to get your product or
  service ready for launch. Also, note any future products or
  services you plan to develop.

- Gatekeepers
  Are there any gatekeepers to your success which lenders or

investors should be aware of? Perhaps you are the local licensee of a product in a defined geographical area, so you only have a business for as long as your licence lasts. And, if that is the case, what plans do you have to minimize any risk that those arrangements might be terminated with little or no notice?

Objective: Products and Services

If they have read this far in your business plan, investors and lenders will be convinced you have identified customers with a real problem they are prepared to spend money fixing, that you have a reasonable chance of those customers buying from you, given the structure of market you operate in, and that you've got the people and organization you need to deliver your organisational goals.

Now you need to make your product or service "real" for investors and lenders.

You introduced the broad concepts already in the Company Overview section – perhaps your product or service is cheaper, faster, lasts longer or has features none of your competitors have.

The Products and Services section is where you prove the claim you set out earlier in your business plan.

Don't just say it's cheaper, explain what's different about your manufacturing process and break down the costing compared to current providers.

Don't just say it lasts longer, explain the testing you've done in some detail and show the side-by-side results.

By the time they finish reading this section, you want investors and lenders to believe your product or service will do everything you say it does, and more. Establishing the credibility of your product or service is your key objective here.

Sales and Marketing: Selling your product or service

People often talk about "Sales" or "Sales and Marketing" to refer to the entire process of landing a new customer.

This is one area of the business plan that is frequently not given the level of attention it deserves, especially in today's highly competitive markets.

100 years ago, creating a product that worked was enough on its own to make some sales and build a business. Demand was far higher than supply and even a third-rate washing machine was better than taking your family's laundry down to the nearest river to wash it by hand.

But just having a good product is no guarantee of success now...and hasn't been for at least 30 years. Nowadays there is vastly more supply in the market than there is demand, forcing prices down and competition up.

The world is very different today.

"Build it and they will come" doesn't work any more

The mentality of "if we build something, we just need to hire some people to sell it and we'll be fine" is still pervasive in too many businesses.

Sometimes, to be fair, it works. For every James Dyson – who built a vacuum cleaner nobody asked him to and became a billionaire – there are millions of people who give up on their dreams and go back to a life they thought they had left behind after discovering world wasn't quite as enthusiastic about their product as they were themselves.

One of the ways to avoid becoming one of those business owners who have to give up their dreams and go back to whatever they did before is to separate the "sales" element from the "marketing" element in how you build your business plan.

There obviously needs to be some linkage between the two, as one process flows into the other. This isn't somewhere you want the two adjacent parts of the customer acquisition process to be speaking a language the other doesn't understand. (Although you might be surprised how often that's exactly what businesses end up with.)

Although people often think sales and marketing are much the same thing, two sides of the same coin perhaps, in reality sales and marketing are two entirely different functions, with different objectives, different skillsets, and different technologies.

The only time the two come pretty close is if you run a pure e-commerce business, selling products and services straight off a website.

But even then, you'll benefit by designing the process of converting a cold lead into a loyal, enthusiastic customer by thinking of sales and marketing as two separate, albeit interlinked, pieces of the jigsaw, rather than being all jumbled up together.

At its heart marketing is about making sure customers know you exist and teeing them up for a sale. However, an absolutely crucial, but often completely forgotten, part of the marketing process is making sure customers who express an interest in dealing with your business are the right customers for you.

At first sight, this might seem a little odd. After all, you want every customer you can get your hands on, don't you? Well, hold on to that thought, we will be back to explore that in a moment or two.

Sales, on the other hand, is about taking the right prospects for your business, namely those prospects who made it through your marketing processes successfully, and helping them make a buying decision that favours your business.

Talk about your product or service differently

Before we get to all that, first we need to look at how you're going to talk about your product or service to make it stand out from your competition.

Note carefully – this is not what makes it different in some practical, physical dimension, which we discussed in the previous section, but rather how you're going to talk about your product or service differently.

And if you think that sounds like the same thing, you have inadvertently fallen into the same trap a lot of businesses fall into.

How you talk about your products is not necessarily going to be what makes it physically different from your competitors. It might be, but it doesn't have to be.

Sometimes, you can even talk about your product in a way that positions it differently, even though it is physically more or less identical to your competitors' products.

The best way to explain this is to give you a couple of examples.

An example of not talking about what made the product different...or at least not directly...was a famous advertisement written by legendary advertising executive David Ogilvy for Rolls-Royce motor cars.

His headline: "At 60 miles an hour the loudest noise in this new Rolls-Royce comes from the electric clock".

What Rolls-Royce actually did was engineer the engine block in such a way as to make it virtually silent even when running at top speed, as well as developing innovative insulation against sound and vibration from the engine, suspension, road rumble and wind noise as the car sped along.

That was what made their product different.

What made David Ogilvy's advertisement one of the most famous ads of all time was the way he talked about what they had done.

He didn't talk about the engine or the suspension or the sound insulation at all...although I'm sure they were marvellous feats of engineering for the time in their own right too.

He talked about the clock being the loudest thing in the car, which put all the other work Rolls-Royce's finest engineers had done so perfectly into context.

At the stroke of David Ogilvy's pen, potential customers knew the engine was virtually silent even though he never mentioned the engine in his headline.

That is the difference between making your product unique, different, and distinctive, which the Rolls-Royce engineers had of course done perfectly...and making your marketing and selling approach unique, different, and distinctive.

By the time you complete this section, you will know exactly how to do that, and you'll understand why this is possibly the most important section of your business plan to get right if you want to run a successful business.

There is another very famous advertisement which is an example of talking about something which is virtually identical for every business in the sector, but still getting an astonishing bump in business on the back of it.

This advertisement was written by another legendary advertising executive – this time Claude Hopkins who took Schlitz beer from a distant number eight in the US beer market to joint first on the back of a series of ads which talked about "All [our] beer is cooled in plate glass rooms, in filtered air. Then the beer is filtered. Then it is sterilized, after being bottled and sealed."

This is an amusing approach because, then as now, that is exactly how every large brewer brewed their beer.

The difference was no other brewer talked about their process in that way.

The genius of Claude Hopkins was to establish a distinctive market positioning just by talking about something commonplace in the industry, but which no other brewer talked about.

So how you talk about your product, and what your product is or does, doesn't have to be exactly the same thing.

In fact, with rare exceptions...James Dyson does talk about his unique vortex vacuum technology, to be fair...it is almost certainly better not to talk about your product purely in terms of its physical features because they are usually the easiest elements to copy.

Instead, you should talk about your product in ways which have the biggest impact on your customers, which brings us to one of the most misunderstood, and most poorly applied, concepts in business, the unique selling proposition, or USP.

Your edge

We spoke about your "edge" earlier in this action guide, and the importance of having something that sets you apart from your competition.

Sometimes people call that edge their USP, or unique selling proposition. I would say a USP is specifically about how you sell your products and services whereas an "edge" might be something else aimed at creating a positive image for your business but not specifically part of the selling process.

Sadly, USP is one of the most misused terms in the business dictionary. Often, what people tell me is their USP is neither unique nor a selling proposition.

They might be factually correct...in fact, they usually are...but customers are not going to forge a path to your door if your promotional materials concentrate on things your customers are not all that interested in.

Many businesses say their USP is something like "founded in 1924". That might be factually correct and hints at some longevity, which potentially opens the door to establishing trustworthiness.

But that's a pretty tenuous link at best. Many businesses have behaved appallingly for long periods of time (looking at you here, Big Tobacco), so longevity is not a guarantee of trustworthiness. "Loansharking since 1924" would not inspire me.

And "founded in 1924" is not unique. Thousands, perhaps hundreds of thousands, of businesses formed in 1924 are still operating today. Furthermore, whatever else "founded in 1924" might be, it's definitely not a selling proposition.

Having "founded in 1924" as your USP is unlikely to do you any harm, but it's hardly going to set the pulses of millions of potential customers raging either.

The cost of an underwhelming USP is that customers you could have sold something to just never come near your business because you didn't give them a compelling reason to do so.

Another common mistake businesses make is to have something they call their USP, but it's completely meaningless because everyone in their industry says the same thing.

For several years now, every insurance broker I speak to tells me their USP is that they "check out the whole market to get you the best price".

Quite frankly, that's the absolute minimum I would expect from a professional insurance broker, otherwise I might as well just call a few random insurance companies myself.

You can add in travel websites which promise to find you the lowest airfare (they all say that) or investment websites which promise to get you the best return for your money (they all say that too).

When everyone in your industry says the same thing, even if it's true for your particular business, it is neither unique nor much of a selling proposition.

The final category of non-USPs to avoid are the sort of USPs someone in the marketing department came up with after one too many caramel lattes late at night.

While the caffeine and sugar were still coursing round their veins, they came up with a strapline for the website which says something like "Inspiring the future through human technology solutions".

I would like to think that was unique, but sadly a lot of businesses claim that sort of meaningless waffle is their USP.

The only purpose statements like that serve is to give me a pretty strong indication that nobody inside that business, and particularly nobody inside their marketing department, has any idea what a USP really is.

What a USP really is

So, if none of those statements are USPs, what is a USP?

The term "unique selling proposition" was coined by the third legendary adman we have mentioned so far in this section. This time it was the work of Rosser Reeves who pretty much set the template for modern TV advertising in the US in the 1950s and 1960s.

Rosser Reeves summed up his approach in a book he wrote in the early 1960s called "Reality in Advertising".

Although this is a lot harder to do now than it was in the early 1960s when Rosser Reeves ruled the advertising waves, it is worth knowing what the gold standard of USP really is, according to his definition.

Just to put this in context, Rosser Reeves was talking about USPs in the context of advertising, which isn't quite what we're doing here.

You're not developing an advertisement at this stage. You're just outlining for investors and lenders the approach you would take to sell your product in the market.

That said, it can be extremely useful to think about how you would get this across in an advertisement to reduce the risk of coming up with meaningless statements like "Inspiring the future through human technology solutions".

That end-goal helps distil out how you would talk about your product or service to real-world customers. And if you can nail that, you will more than satisfy any interest in the subject your investors and lenders might have.

According to Rosser Reeves, there are three elements to a great USP:

1. You must make a proposition to the customer, not just engage in product puffery or show-window advertising. The proposition should say "buy this product for this specific benefit".

   A good example of this being done badly is the non-USP "Inspiring the future through human technology solutions" mentioned above" which isn't a proposition at all. Claims of "the best office cleaning service in the country" similarly fall foul of this element as that is just puffery.

2. The proposition must be one the competition does not offer...or cannot offer.

   Claude Hopkins' Schlitz beer advertising is a great example of how to forge a sustainable USP using a facet of the product or service no-one else in your industry talks about it (ie it's a proposition the competition does not offer).

3. The proposition must "move the masses", that is, it must be strong enough to attract new customers as well as keeping existing customers loyal.

   Saying something everyone else says, like the cheap flight

websites which all claim to find the cheapest fares, or something without a real impetus to it, such as "founded in 1924", are extremely unlikely to move the masses to do anything very much, never mind keeping existing customers loyal.

Of course, the sort of USP Rosser Reeves talked about was much easier when there were only three major car brands and two major washing machine manufacturers. It was never easy to build a great USP, but nowadays it's harder than ever.

That doesn't mean you shouldn't try, though. And you can certainly do better than "founded in 1924" without trying terribly hard.

Explain to investors and lenders what your USP is. If they say "wow, that's quite a proposition", the more likely it is they will give you the funding you need and, in turn, the more likely it is your business will be successful when it is unleashed on the real world.

Your competitors

A key part of building a great USP is being really clear about what your competition says and does.

Don't be like all those insurance brokers with non-USPs exactly the same as every other insurance broker. Find out what your competitors say and make sure whatever you say is distinctive and as unique as possible.

As part of this exercise, make sure you check out all your less-obvious sources of competition, because you need to neutralise them too...in fact they can often be more difficult competitors to beat than the obvious ones, as we will see in a few moments.

Back in the Market Analysis section of your business plan we identified your major competitors to help give potential investors and lenders some context about your industry.

Now it's time to take a closer look at not just who they are, but also exactly what they're up to.

You want to know how they deliver their product or service, how they talk about what they do to potential customers, how fast they are growing, how successful they are and how you can secure a different position in the market from whatever position they seem to be trying to occupy.

Once you have done that, you should be a little clearer on your messaging, but you still need to consider the precise activities you are going to carry out to make sure customers find you.

It's all very well having a great product. But however great it is, that counts for nothing if nobody knows your business exists. That's the first step in getting anyone to buy your product.

Attracting customers

Let's get this clear up-front. This section will not help you unless your product or service is as good as it can possibly be.

You need to do everything you can inside your business to have a great story to tell potential customers. Even if you make a sale once, with a poor product or indifferent service, nobody will be coming back to buy a second time.

A business which has to constantly find new customers because their product is of poor quality or their service experience lacking, sooner or later runs out of people to sell to who haven't already been disappointed by their previous experiences of dealing with this business.

However, having a great product and a great story to tell is only part of the battle.

Unless you are in the highly unusual situation of creating an entirely new market with the launch of your product or service, which only happens once or twice in a generation, there are only two ways you can get customers to buy from you.

Either you need to persuade people who are currently buying from your competitors to switch their purchases over to you, or you need to persuade people who have not bought products and services like yours historically to start caring enough about what you sell to start buying them now.

If your potential customers are already buying a similar product from one of your competitors, investors and lenders will want to know how you plan to win business away from your competition. (Pro tip: this should not just be about cutting prices, which is the beginning and end of what most businesses consider.)

Not only that, but you also need to consider how would counter any tactics existing suppliers might deploy to win back the customers you tempted away.

This is just one reason why trying to win business purely on the basis of being cheaper than the current supplier only invites the lazy response of that supplier undercutting you in turn, after which you to retaliate once more, and for that cycle to keep repeating itself until neither of you is making any money.

Equally, if you unveil a dramatically improved product or service, it would be unwise to expect your competitors to stand by while their most valuable customers walk out the door.

You need to think carefully about how you will get your message out and make the sales you need.

Avoid these common mistakes

Even if you think your product or service is unique in your market, there are two important...but remarkably common...mistakes businesses make which can negatively impact your marketing plan.

Firstly, the "build it and they will come" principle.

Despite what you might believe if you have seen the Kevin Costner film "Field of Dreams", people do not actually do this.

The most spectacular recent example of this is Quibi which burned through $1.75 billion of investor capital to create a product nobody wanted to buy. But there are plenty of other, less public, examples of this phenomenon in businesses large and small across the country every year.

Had it not been for the previously stellar track records of the people who set up Quibi, they would never have raised such an enormous sum of money to achieve so little.

Their reputations opened doors which would not be open to you and me. But for normal mortals, you can't really spend millions, or even billions, setting up a business, open the doors at 9am one Monday morning and expect there to be queues around the block outside.

Now and again, someone does this and becomes an "overnight success", of course. Their achievements get written up in business magazines as if the company founder was a genius, but the truth is they just got lucky. They were half a human hair's breadth away from bankruptcy at the moment they threw their doors open.

If you are going to rely on luck making you a success, Las Vegas casinos probably offer better odds of success than ploughing everything you own into a new business venture without doing your homework first.

Secondly, even if you think you have no competitors, and even if you are correct in your assessment (which, by the way, you're probably not...as you'll see in a moment), don't discount the possibility that customers might choose to do nothing at all.

Inertia, or habit if you prefer that term, has a bigger role to play in sales than most businesses would like to think.

In fact, strange as it may seem, it is usually easier to switch people from their current supplier for something they already buy than it is to get people to start buying something they've never bought before.

At least people who buy products and services broadly similar to yours care about the problem your product or service solves. You know they have some degree of positive feelings towards that category of products which you can work with.

The challenge of getting people to buy something they have never bought from anyone before is surprisingly daunting.

You might imagine this would be easier than tempting people away from their existing suppliers, but it isn't. Even if your product is great and your USP exceptional, those prospective customers have formed, and deeply embedded within their psyche, a habit of "not buying" products like yours over many years.

Switching any deeply ingrained habit in completely the opposite direction is going to bring some significant challenges, not least of which is to get your prospective customers to start caring enough about products like yours to give you a try-out, despite never having cared about them up till now.

It's hard, but it isn't impossible – as long as you do your homework and think about how you'll approach your target market. Plenty of businesses have taken on exactly these challenges over the years and succeeded.

In fact, this is another great reason to create an annual business plan. It gives you the chance to think about all the issues, challenges and opportunities you might encounter and formulate a plan to deal with them long before you spend a boatload of cash you can't get back and taken financial risks you didn't need to take.

But you can do it. It's been done millions of times throughout history.

When I think back to my early years at work, nobody quaffed cappuccinos or flat whites, used beard oil (or even had beards), or carried a computer around in their pocket all the time.

Yet today none of those things are unusual or exceptional in any way (although I still don't understand beard oil, personally).

In all those sectors, someone made people care about things they had never cared about before and made a fortune on the back of changing the habits of millions of people.

But all those businesses had to conquer the toughest competitor of all – inertia.

And you will have to do the same - either the inertia that keeps your target customers locked into the habit of buying from their current supplier or the inertia that comes from potential customers having got into the habit of not spending money on products and services like yours.

Never convince yourself you have "no competition". Even if that just means getting people to care enough about your product or service to buy something they have never bought before – the competition of inertia, you might say – you have always got competition.

The less-obvious competition

Often your toughest competition won't come from the most obvious place – businesses in the same industry as you.

Let's say you are in the commuter airline business, taking people on short hops from your local airport to the nearest big city or to a regional hub airport for an onward flight with a major airline.

Maybe you run the only airline flying to that destination from your local airport. But does that mean you have no competition?

Absolutely not. For distances up to a few hundred miles, your competition is not just other airlines, although they might be a source of competition too.

Rather, your toughest competition is probably people driving themselves to the nearest big city instead of flying, ridesharing with a work colleague who happens to be going to the same place on the same day or catching the train instead.

You might run the only airline on the route, but flying is not the only way to get from your town to the nearest big city. There's probably a dozen or more ways to do that.

What's more, all the other ways customers can get to their destination without using your commuter airline might offer benefits you don't, all of which you need to neutralize if you're going to sell seats on your planes.

Some people...me, for example...hate driving and would jump on an airplane to make that journey at the drop of the hat.

Even then, if it was going to cost me $20 in fuel to drive or $300 to fly, I might decide to put my normal preference on one side and save $280 by taking a leisurely drive instead.

The upshot is you have always got competition. Even if you think you haven't got any competition because you run the only airline flying that route.

The long-haul airline business is quite different. If you want to get from London to New York in under 10 hours, your only realistic competition is other airlines. There are no other modes of transport, at least for now, which can do that.

So British Airways competes with American Airlines, Delta and the other big airlines which fly the same route in, by and large, identical Boeing and Airbus aircraft.

That is a very different competitive landscape than the one a commuter airline faces.

British Airways competes purely with other airlines on the London to New York route, a commuter airline has dozens of potential competitors, probably very few, or none, of them other airlines.

For that reason, you need to delve quite deeply into how your customers behave in the real world to spot your competitors, particularly the less-obvious ones.

Building your marketing plan

By this stage, you know what makes your product or service unique…or at least relatively so…and how you are going to talk about that uniqueness and distinctiveness in a way that will make potential customers want to buy from you via a compelling USP.

You have also checked out your competitors (both obvious and non-obvious) so you can position yourself differently to them. And you have given some thought to how you will counter your competitors' attempts to hang onto their current customers and make it hard for you to tempt them away.

The next step is to take this knowledge and start building your marketing plan.

At its simplest, marketing is how the big, wide world out there even knows your business and your products exist.

This is a lot harder than it used to be as there is so much more noise in the marketplace and so many more different ways of getting marketing messages across than there used to be.

But it is essential you find a way, otherwise you are relying on pure luck for customers to walk through your door or randomly find your website. And, as we have already noted, pure luck isn't generally the most reliable approach to building a sustainable business.

The points you need to address for potential investors and lenders in this section are:

- Your positioning relative to your competitors – why should customers come to you rather than another business providing a similar product or service? Will you offer, for example:

  - Lower prices
  - Superior quality
  - Superior service

- If you think you have no competitors, firstly you are almost certainly wrong and secondly, even if you are right, you need to persuade people to care about something they've got through life to this point without caring about before now.

  You need to show investors and lenders how you will ignite your target market's enthusiasm to care enough to spend their money with you.

- The specific promotional methods you intend to use to get the word out about your product or service. Which, among the hundreds of potential ways of promoting your business, will you be majoring in, at least at first - online advertising, social media marketing, press ads in your local newspaper, radio commercials, billboards, etc, etc.

- In this section you should also clarify the metrics you intend to use in evaluating whether your marketing is working (leads generated, social media reach, website visitors, sales made, coupons redeemed, etc).

- Finally, consider laying out a graphic of your marketing process to help investors and lenders understand how the economics of your customer acquisition process work, and link that into your sales processes, which we will cover in a moment, to tell the complete story of how a customer goes from never having heard of your business to making a purchase.

In all this, there are no hard-and-fast rules that always work, irrespective of sector, customer base or geography. Anyone who tells you they have a guaranteed way to do your marketing and bring in new customers doesn't know what they're talking about.

The good news, however, is that if you engage with the thinking processes above, you will find it easier to make the sales your business needs and you will grow faster and more profitably than your competitors because you have done the homework that many businesses do not.

That way, you dramatically increase the odds your business will achieve everything you dreamed of when you first opened your doors.

Getting your marketing right is an important first step in making a sale, but the job of making a sale isn't even half done yet.

Qualifying a marketing lead

The next part of the sales and marketing process is qualifying a lead. This means making sure a potential customer is the right customer for your business.

"What?", you might say, "I need every customer I can get. I'm not about to turn anyone away!"

Sadly, you'd be wrong to say that.

Whenever I see a business in real trouble, it is often because they thought it wasn't necessary to qualify the leads generated by their marketing activities and took on every customer who came their way without considering the consequences.

Think about it - is everyone who clicks on one of your ads, sends in a coupon or calls your office a genuine lead for your business?

Sometimes, maybe even most of the time if the marketing gods are smiling on you, they are. But remarkably often, they're not.

For digital advertising, click fraud (where automated bots "click" ads as part of a scam) can be a big issue – not every click is a genuine potential customer. Even without ad fraud, people click links by mistake, especially on mobile devices when large fingers are prodding away at small screens.

It is also not uncommon to misspell another company's name and end up on your website by mistake. Or for someone to mindlessly scroll through the internet on their lunchbreak and go down a rabbit hole of some sort which brings them to your website without any real intention of buying anything.

This isn't just a problem for digital advertising. It applies to any lead-generation process, online or offline.

Some of the people who wander into your shop are only doing so to get out of the rain.

Some of your inbound calls will be wrong numbers or callers who think your company sells something it doesn't.

Not everyone who clips a coupon wants to buy something, especially if you offer a free gift or an incentive for sending in a response. Sometimes they just want that freebie and have no intention of becoming a customer at all.

Even referrals – the golden chalice of lead generation for most businesses – are not always the right sort of customer for you, for a whole variety of reasons.

The list goes on and on, but the bottom line is that not every click, call, coupon, referral, or lead, however generated, will be a lead you should want to pursue, or could afford to serve profitably even if you do.

This is even before we consider issues like whether the enquirer has the budget for your services, the authority to purchase them, works in an industry you serve, or is based in a geographic location you support.

And don't forget the biggest reason of all for not wanting to deal with a potential customer…some people customers have "trouble" written all over them from Day 1, based on their attitude, how they talk to your staff and the evidence of how often they keep to their commitments.

Even if potential customers pass those hurdles, long before you think about making a sale, you need to set some criteria for what you would consider a "real lead".

For example, if people don't download the free report they're offered when they land on your website, you might decide they are unlikely to be a serious sales prospect. More likely they were just casual browsers.

There is nothing wrong with that, and of course some casual browsers come back to purchase something at a later date. But you need to think, as part of your marketing and sales plan, what steps would a customer need to take to demonstrate their interest in your product, sufficient for you to expend a fair chunk of expensive sales resources on it.

You don't want your sales team chasing leads with a 1-in-1000 chance of turning into a sale when they could be chasing leads with a 1-in-4 chance of making a sale instead.

In every industry, your sales team is far too expensive a resource to fritter away on 1-in-a-1000 sales prospects. The laws of economics dictate you will be out of business long before you land enough prospects to create a profitable business.

The marketing qualification process is what gets you down from chasing 1-in-1000 prospects to focus in on the more sensible 1-in-4 prospects instead.

It might seem counterintuitive to, as some would see it, put steps in the way of making a sale. But this is vital if you want to avoid burning through your sales and marketing budget for very little return.

The steps should not be so big as to put people off, but you need to get them to do something to evidence their commitment – download a report, agree to a product demonstration, accept a free trial of your product or service, or whatever might be appropriate in your sector.

If they take a tiny step to demonstrate their interest, they might well be realistic sales prospects, but even then, especially in a B2B environment, we don't yet know if they have the authority or the budget to buy.

Your sales team will check some of those issues when they get to talk with each potential new customer, but you might also want to do some other basic checks as part of your qualification process before handing the lead across to your sales team.

You might check their address to make sure they are in a geographic location you serve. You could download a copy of their accounts to make sure they are large enough to be likely to have a budget for your services. Or you could do a Google search on the business to understand more about their future plans and check their social media output for clues about their operations.

Sadly, there are no approaches guaranteed to work in every industry with every type of customer.

The key, though, is thinking through very carefully what your qualification process would be.

Get quite specific on what it is a potential customer would need to do to signal a degree of genuine interest and what your business would then do to cross-check or validate that interest before deciding this was a genuine prospect for your sales team to try to bring over the finishing line as a new customer.

Your Sales Plan

Let's recap the sales and marketing process so far.

It started with an enquiry or expression of interest of some sort, either online or offline. Someone clicked on your website, called your 24-hour customer service line or did something else to indicate their potential interest in what you have to offer.

You then got the enquirer to do something to demonstrate they were serious prospects and not just tire-kickers.

And you have done some cross-checking to make sure this new enquiry has a realistic prospect of turning into a sale.

With that in the bag, it's time to move from your marketing plan – making sure people have heard about your business and qualifying out those who, for whatever reason, don't appear to be serious prospects –

and start to build a sales plan, where you take enquiries with a realistic prospect of turning into a sale and start selling.

Again, you need to think through the processes you intend to follow and the mechanisms, strategies and techniques you plan to deploy to get prospects who expressed an interest in your product or service, and passed your qualification process, over the line to become buyers.

Common ways of doing that include:

- Outbound calling in response to a clipped coupon or registration on your website

- Adding them to an email sequence of some sort, designed to warm them up for the sale or even, ultimately, make the sale itself

- In-person meetings with decision-makers in your target customers

- Webinars

- Product demonstrations (online or offline)

- Free 14 or 30-day trials of your service which automatically roll over to a regular-priced subscription at the end of the trial period unless cancelled

Just as important as the method you choose, you need to be clear about who is going to make the sale?

There is cold calling, webinars, product demonstrations and client presentations to be done, and a sales team someone needs to keep tabs on.

Who is going to manage the people and the process? Perhaps it's yourself, or maybe you intend bringing someone in to do that job for you.

Either way, your business plan needs to explain how your sales and marketing teams are resourced appropriately to find the customers you need.

Once more, this is where you need to think things through from an investor or lender's perspective.

It will take a lot of persuasion for lenders or investors to believe that in a few moments here and there during the business day a business owner will bring in sales of $10million a year all by themselves without a sales team.

If you intend making all your sales through social media but your budget for Facebook ads is tiny and your organisation chart doesn't show a social media manager or PPC specialist in there somewhere, they're going to doubt your business model.

Investors and lenders understand there are no prefect decisions here, and many different ways of getting to the same ends.

But you need to convince them that your sales and marketing plans are sensible, realistic and adequately resourced because that's the first step in generating the sales income you need to cover your costs and make a profit.

In particular, make sure any budgets – for revenue generated, salaries, bonuses and benefits for your salespeople, and any investments you need to make in marketing to generate leads for your sales team to close – are specific, realistic, and thought through carefully.

Talk about process

Savvy investors and lenders, and in the absence of any other information, you should presume they all are, will see through any smokescreens placed in their way.

Your investors and lenders will do the basic maths involved, so don't get caught out. Unless you explain to them exactly what you plan to do, they will make up their own numbers and reach their own conclusions about how realistic they think your plans are.

Don't risk them coming to a significantly more pessimistic conclusion than you have – if that happens, you're very unlikely to see any funding coming your way.

Set out your sales and marketing process in sequence so investors and lenders can follow along with your logic, rather than risk them deploying their own.

For example, you might describe your sales and marketing process like this:

- We spend $1000 a month on Google Ads, which brings us 100 leads a month…

- We offer a free report to people who end up on our website from those ads. Based on past performance, about half of them will download our free report...

- For enquirers who download the report, we check out their company financials and make sure they have revenues of at least $10m per year. Given the nature of our services, it is rare that a business smaller than that would need or could afford our solution...

- Then we pass the lead to our sales team, who convert one prospect in five into a customer with an average order value of $100,000 each.

- On average, therefore, we expect to make sales of $1m per month (one-in-five of the 50 people who download the report is 10 people. 10 people at $100,000 each is $1m).

Naturally, your precise situation will be different, but in a few short sentences like the ones above, potential investors and lenders can understand exactly how you are going to find potential customers and make the sales you need.

This often works best as a graphic, or a flowchart, but even as a handful of written paragraphs the key assumptions jump out.

More importantly – because, after all, your business plan is more for you than it is for external investors and lenders – you have also built up a picture you can use to track your sales and marketing team's performance going forward.

If your 100 leads cost $2000 next month instead of $1000, that should flag up something to look at.

Similarly, if your 1-in-5 conversion slips to 1-in-7 or your average order value slips to $70,000 instead of $100,000.

In less than half a page of text you have clarified exactly what needs to happen to reach your sales target of $1m per month and if any of those targets start to drift away from your initial assumptions, you know exactly where to look, and what needs fixing.

It's not just bad news you need to look out for. Good news can present challenges at least as hard...sometimes harder.

Imagine your sales team starts converting enquiries at the rate of 1-in-3 instead of 1-in-5. All things being equal, you will need to hire more staff, invest in your operations, and prepare for a larger volume of customer service enquiries.

By seeing the impact of those changes early in the process, you have an opportunity to prepare for increased activity in your business a few weeks or months later, depending on the length of your sales cycle, when the sales come through.

You can plan ahead, staff up and invest, if necessary, to keep everything on track and make sure your customers get exactly the quality of product and service you promised.

You're not running around like a scalded cat, watching semi-helpless as your business lurches from one crisis to the next in the face of an unexpected onslaught of customer orders.

So do the math for your investors and lenders. Don't leave it to them to make up their own stories.

Set out, in clear and simple terms, exactly how you intend to go from a "cold" enquiry to a sale and give as much evidence as possible to demonstrate your assumptions are reasonable.

Investors and lenders are always interested in making sure the assumptions and calculations behind how you plan to build your sales revenue appear sensible and are reasonably likely to come to fruition, if for no other reason than because that is ultimately how they're going to make sure they get their money back.

Don't wait until a potential lender or investor points out an error in your business model. Work through the logic, check the math and make sure there are no flaws in your thinking.

Finally, with the metrics you have used to create your sales and marketing plan, make sure you set up a reporting system to track the performance of your sales and marketing team on a weekly, monthly, quarterly and annual basis so you'll get an early warning if anything changes.

Of all the many elements of your business plan, this is the set of metrics you want to stay closest too, especially early on. If sales revenues are not coming in on schedule, it is unlikely there will be much else you can do to get your bottom line back on track.

Once the plan is clearly working as intended, and the revenue targets you set are broadly being delivered, you can afford to divert some of your attention elsewhere.

But make sure your sales and marketing machine is running like clockwork first. If the sales revenues are not coming in bang on schedule, the likelihood of you ultimately delivering on your business plan is low.

So, expect professional investors and lenders to be very interested in the Sales and Marketing section of your business plan. Make sure you are fully prepared.

Sales and Marketing: Must-haves

- Process
  Set out the process from beginning to end. Clarity is your goal here – don't just tell investors and lenders you will spend $10,000 on marketing and make sales of $1million while being skimpy on the details. You have not yet earned the level of trust you need to get away with that.

- Product pricing and margins
  Using the per unit financials you outlined in the Products and Services section (added value, gross margin, etc), work through the numbers for each main product or service line you sell, assuming you hit the sales revenue targets set out in the Sales and Marketing section of your business plan.

  Illustrate how, for example, your selling price of $5 per unit on Product A, multiplied up across the one million units a year you intend to produce, gives you a $5 million income stream from Product A, at a gross margin of 40%. (You will pick these numbers up again when you come to the Financials section shortly.)

- Potential options
  If your business model allows for a range of different solutions eg a bronze, silver and gold plan, or a sale with or without the five year extended warranty plan, be clear what proportion of customers will select each and show how each option benefits your bottom line.

- Building confidence
  Some business owners are a bit nervous about "sharing their

secrets", and you might want to hold back some of the fine details until you have a signed contract in your hand, but if investors and lenders can't see how you plan to deliver on your revenue line, or don't feel your assumptions are realistic, they'll bail out pretty quickly. Make sure you tell them enough to give them the confidence that your plans are realistic.

- Competitors
  Explain who your major competitors are and summarise their strengths and weaknesses to give an idea of the competitive landscape for your products and services.

- Standing out
  Show how your chosen approach fits into that market structure. Explain what you do differently and why that is more likely to generate the revenues you need than whatever the rest of the market does at the moment.

  If no-one else in your market offers a 30-day free trial, that could well be a winner. If everyone does, you might need to think again because you will just fade into the greyness of a mass of near-identical offers, making it almost impossible to stand out.

- Make it real
  Build on external data sources, such as the industry reports you introduced in the Market Analysis section of the business plan, to show the current size of the market and explain why and how you see the market changing over the life of your business plan.

- What sectors and customers are you targeting, and why?
  Describe your ideal customer – and, perhaps more importantly,

the sectors or businesses you won't serve and why (eg too small, too far away, cost of customising your product is too high for different regulatory environments, etc).

- Cost budgets
  Include cost budgets for each major cost heading in your sales and marketing plans. If your modelling says you need 10 salespeople to sign up new clients based on your sales and marketing plans, make sure you include the full costs of salaries and benefits for those 10 people.

  If you need to spend $100,000 on advertising to generate the level of enquiries you need to reach your sales targets, make sure that is in your plan too.

- Marketing collateral
  While it is by no means compulsory, if you happen to have a worked-up visual of some marketing materials or a wireframe of your proposed website, that does no harm. That can help lenders or investors who have trouble visualising what the end-result might look like understand your proposal better.

  But don't work up marketing materials, or even full marketing campaigns, purely for the benefit of potential lenders or investors. It's nice for them to see if you've got something to show them, but it is not essential to their decision-making process.

  Just sell them on your vision, passion, the quality of your products or services and your well-thought-out plan for generating a flood of sales by offering a solution that is different and better than other providers in the market.

Objective: Sales and Marketing

After reading the Sales and Marketing section of your business plan, investors and lenders should be convinced that:

a) You have a winning proposition to get potential customers beating a path to your business, and

b) When potential customers arrive there, you have a solid system for taking cold leads and turning them into loyal customers.

You also need to be clear about what you don't do. In many ways that is more important than what you are going to do.

No successful business can serve every sector of every market profitability and only amateurs even try. Be clear where you are focusing your efforts.

As you get more and more successful, you can always expand your offer and move into adjacent sectors. But only do it on the back of being successful in one sector first, not as a consolation prize for failing in another sector – those decisions rarely work in the long-term.

Make sure you leave investors and lenders with a clear understanding of how you are going to drive the revenues you need into your business.

Capital Investment: Investing to win

No matter what you propose to invest in, investors and lenders expect to see a clear rationale for what you want to buy and an understanding of how that will benefit the business – especially in terms of improving profitability and cash flow.

This is important because usually a business can't un-do major capital investments very easily...and certainly not inexpensively.

Once the contract is signed, you are generally stuck with the investment, for good or ill. So, investors and lenders need to be convinced their cash isn't going down some bottomless money pit but will instead play a major role in creating a more profitable business, better positioned for the future.

Even the best-run businesses get caught out by capital investments that go completely off the rails, so potential investors and lenders naturally see this as an area of risk. They will want to be comfortable your proposal represents good value to the business and provides a safe home for their cash.

Capital investment appraisal gets extremely complicated really quickly, but for the purpose of this section of your business plan, you need to:

- Be very clear on the exact timing of any payments to suppliers as they tend to be significant items in your cash flow forecast. When buying expensive equipment, it is not uncommon for contracts to require a significant cash deposit on signing the contract, even though the asset you're buying won't, in all probability, be installed for several months yet.

While the total cost is important, you also need to highlight when your cash flow will be impacted by any deposits and stage payments built into the contract.

Equally your final payment might be conditional on some commissioning tests to demonstrate the contractual performance standards have been met by the supplier. Make sure all those subtleties are clear in the narrative in this section and appear appropriately on your cash flow forecasts.

- Explain the benefits of the proposed investment – what opportunities will the investment open up for your business you can't get any other way?

- Set out how the proposed investment will generate a positive RoI (Return on Investment), over and above the cost of the asset and any associated financing costs, over a reasonable timespan.

- Demonstrate the steps you have taken to ensure the proposed investment will do what the supplier claims and outline the options you have if it doesn't work as promised.

What right of redress do you have if your new investment doesn't dramatically increase throughput in your factory, for example, or if you don't see the substantial manufacturing cost savings you were promised?

Quantify the benefits

Often the clearest way to demonstrate the positive impact of a proposed capital investment is to carve out the relevant sections of your operation and show the current position side-by-side with the post-investment scenario.

Don't just say the investment will make your operations more efficient. Investors and lenders will take that as read. Otherwise, why would you be making the investment?

The key is to quantify how much more efficient your business will become in some meaningful way – the increase in units produced per day, or the reduction in unit labour costs as a result of greater automation, for example.

And if an investment is intended to make your business more efficient, what will you do differently with the benefit of those greater efficiencies?

More efficiency is worthwhile in its own right of course, but will you just siphon off the extra cash, or will you pay down debt quicker, open up new markets, or invest the savings in a push for increased market share, perhaps?

The possibilities might not literally be endless, but there are a range of perfectly reasonable things you could do, so be clear about your intentions.

You need to convince investors and lenders that the upside from investing their money in a new asset of some description will be far greater than the cost of buying and financing it.

Accountants and financial advisors use complex formulas to calculate Return on Investment for large capital investment projects, using an approach called Discounted Cash Flow (DCF) analysis.

A DCF model draws on a number of factors over and above the cost of the asset itself, such as the expected life of the asset, the timing of the project cash flows, the efficiency savings generated, the impact of tax write-offs, forecast interest rates for the expected useful life of the asset, and a range of other considerations.

Although not all investors and lenders will insist on a full DCF calculation, if you are asked to provide one, this gets complicated very quickly, so even if you're writing most of your business plan yourself, I'd encourage you to get a CPA or financial advisor to work out the DCF calculations for you. They can be quite a challenge for a non-expert, with many potential missteps along the way for the unwary.

However, although this is complicated for a non-expert, a DCF calculation is a fairly simple job for a financial professional and should not represent a significant cost to your business.

If an investor or lender insists on a full DCF analysis, the cost of a professional to work out the investment RoI will more than pay for itself by demonstrating to investors and lenders, in terms they understand, why your proposed investment is a sound project they should back.

Lease or buy?

So far, this section has focused on the traditional model of securing finance to make an asset purchase.

Even if you end up doing something slightly different, as we will explore in this section, you should always do a full, traditional capital investment appraisal to set the baseline against which you can compare other options.

However, if you are contemplating an asset purchase of any sort, at a minimum, your business plan should also include an analysis of whether leasing that same asset is financially more beneficial than buying it outright.

Whichever you decide to do, investors and lenders are only going to ask if you have considered leasing options anyway, so you might as well score some extra points for being sharp enough to give them the answer before they ask the question.

Again, this can also get quite complicated, so some expert financial support might be helpful here too.

But you can do a "quick and dirty" analysis without too much difficulty if you just map out the different cash flows over the life of the asset under both a "buy outright" scenario and a lease option.

This is probably easier to explain with an example.

Imagine you buy a piece of machinery costing $500,000. You expect this asset to last for five years before needing to be replaced, so one way to think of your $500,000 investment is as a cost of $100,000 a year over the five years you expect to use it for.

To make things slightly more complicated, but as a reflection of what is often likely to happen in the real world, let's also imagine you could sell the machine as scrap for $50,000 at the end of five years.

Obviously, that can only be an estimate at the planning stage. None of us can know for sure what the scrap value of any asset in five years' time will be, so don't be overly optimistic.

And, of course, some major investments, like IT systems, have a scrap value of close to zero at the end of their useful life as technology moves on fast. So only include the prospect of selling your asset at the end of its life if that is a realistic expectation.

Going back to our example, if you factor in the scrap value, your net cost now drops to $450,000 in total over five years (ie $500,000 up-front investment less $50,000 scrap value). Put another way, you could see that as a net cost of $90,000 a year (ie the $450,000 net cost divided by five years).

That gives an "rough cut" idea of a baseline cost of this asset, ignoring the cost of finance for the moment and, even without a full traditional capital investment appraisal, this method can help as a comparator for other options you might want to consider.

Manufacturers of expensive equipment nearly always have some sort of in-house financing available for what they sell. This is good business for them as it means they sell more equipment, as well as making a bit of extra margin for themselves on the finance deal along the way.

There are also plenty of third-party lenders who will finance capital equipment purchases. Sometimes their rates are competitive, sometimes they're not.

I generally recommend asking the manufacturer about the financing options they offer, alongside a couple of third-party providers to make sure you get a fair spread of alternatives. In practice nowadays, it is rare for costs to vary much between providers as the finance market is highly competitive, but you never know, so it is worth checking.

For the purposes of our illustration, let's say the manufacturer offers "nothing down" finance and an $80,000 annual leasing cost over the five-year life of the asset.

Now you're comparing a lease cost of $400,000 against a $450,000 cost if you bought the asset for cash.

That isn't as odd as it might sound at first.

Manufacturers generally have a much better idea of what one of their five-year-old machines will be worth than their customers because it's their business to know.

And manufacturers often have routes to markets most of their customers do not – it's quite common for equipment manufacturers to export the five-year-old, but still serviceable, equipment they take back at the end of lease terms in major Western nations to developing countries.

There, even a five-year-old piece of machinery which is seen as out of date in a major Western economy might be a significant step up from the 40-year-old kit they have been using up till now.

Understand the tax implications

The other complication when comparing the cost of leasing an asset against the option of buying the asset outright for cash are the tax breaks you get, or don't get, depending on which type of financing you choose.

It is important to take appropriate professional advice in your own jurisdiction, but, for example, sometimes leasing costs are wholly allowable against a corporate tax bill in the same accounting year the lease payments are made, but amortization charges on capital assets have to be claimed on some different schedule, either more or less favourable.

On the other hand, some governments try to encourage businesses investment by giving valuable up-front tax breaks for new machinery.

A business might get the full cost of a capital investment written off against their tax bill in the year the machine is installed, even though the business might not pay the full price in that accounting year, for example.

Be sure to get appropriate specialist advice on this subject, but the important point here is that whether leasing or buying is the better option depends as much on tax regulations in your jurisdiction as it does on the physical cash flows (both inward and outward) of your planned investment.

My advice is usually not to get too hung up on whether you lease or buy a piece of equipment. Either way you get the investment you want, so this should be a fairly dispassionate decision based on the cash flows over the useful life of the asset (including any pre-installation deposits and any scrap value at the end of the asset's useful life).

Strictly speaking, as we already mentioned, this should be done using a sophisticated appraisal technique called discounted cash flow analysis (DCF) which your CPA or financial advisor can help you with.

Even without a DCF model, one of the options usually comes out as clearly much better than the other if you just add up the cash flows in and out of your business and compare one option to another. Just make sure you reflect the tax position properly as that is often key to the economics of lease or buy decisions.

And if you're anxious about getting high-powered tax advice (at least in the early days of you figuring this out, I'd always advise taking appropriate professional advice before signing contracts or becoming committed to a long-term agreement), don't worry too much.

My experience is that if someone is selling an option which has a more beneficial tax treatment, usually you won't be able to shut them up about the benefit of their solution over other solutions on the market.

They will also generally be happy to work out the comparison between leasing and buying for you because that gets them one step closer to making a sale.

However you pay for your capital investment, what's important in your business plan is that you set out the timing of all the cash flows very clearly and show the total cost of the asset over its anticipated useful working life.

The final point on this subject is to remember that, by and large, you want to have as much of the cash flow happening as late in the cycle as possible.

A 20% up-front deposit for a piece of machinery that will take a year to build is dead money for your business, whereas lease payments that don't start until the machine is delivered is likely to be much better for your cash flow, and hence your Return on Investment calculation, even if the overall costs are broadly similar.

If you have a DCF model to show lenders or investors, it won't do any harm. But unless you are making an investment worth millions of dollars, the sort of analysis you can do yourself, with the aid of your suppliers and lease finance providers, is a good starting point for most "in principle" discussions with investors and lenders.

Any lenders or lenders who wants a more in-depth analysis, or a full DCF appraisal, will be sure to ask. But I rarely see a full-blown DCF analysis more often than one or twice a year, and then only generally for multimillion-dollar, multi-year projects with significant ongoing costs. So, don't let all the technicalities which swirl around capital investment appraisal techniques faze you too much.

Set out the costs and the timescales. Make sure they are clearly itemised in your cash flow projections so that lenders and lenders fully understand the investment proposal you're asking them to support.

For most investors and lenders, this will be enough, especially for early-stage discussions about your plans.

Capital Investment – Must-haves

- The asset itself
  Describe the proposed investment, what it is, what it does and the basis for selecting this asset over any of the other options (including the option of doing nothing).

- Return on investment
  Set out your Return on Investment (RoI) calculation showing the bottom-line impact of making the investment. Make sure you include any ongoing expenditure in your RoI calculation, such annual service agreements, or scheduled maintenance fees.

- Cash flows
  The precise amounts and timing of any outgoing cash flows, including details of any initial deposits, stage payments, upfront lease payments and so on, together with any ongoing liabilities such as service costs and maintenance charges.

- DCF model
  A copy of your DCF modelling from your accountant or financial advisor, if you have one (but don't sweat it too much if you don't).

- Lease or buy analysis
  Set out your decision as to leasing or buying the equipment concerned and show the financial case for both, leading to your conclusion to go down one route or the other.

Final word of advice

With capital expenditure, probably more than any other element of your business plan, be careful you are making what will always be a substantial investment for solid business reasons.

Sometimes businesses get so caught up in the emotions of their decision and the momentum that generates means they start to lose their sense of perspective and ultimately drift into what turns out to be an unwise investment.

It is never presented like that, of course. But more often than you might think, the net impact to a business of a "shiny new toy" is neutral to negative.

People get wrapped up in the emotion of the asset purchase and find all sorts of reasons to keep spending the cash even when it becomes clear to more impartial observers that the prospect of any meaningful impact on the bottom line has become remote.

That rarely leads to good long-term outcomes. Making capital investments is a common source of "decide in haste, repent at leisure" decisions.

Once you are locked in to giving away a share of your business or you have drawn down a multi-year bank loan secured against your family home to finance a major asset purchase, it's too late to back out if that investment decision later turns out to have been unwise.

Challenge any investment proposals hard up-front. Any substantial investment should be paying back its cost many times over to give you a margin for error in case not everything turns out as perfectly as the salesperson for the manufacturer said it would.

Get someone external to act as devil's advocate if you have to, but push hard to make sure you understand the benefits of the investment and satisfy yourself there's enough of a net positive impact on your business bottom line to make any investment worthwhile.

As best you can, don't let your heart over-rule your head.

Objective: Capital Investment

This section may not apply to you but, if part of your business plan involves making a large capital investment, you need to convince investors and lenders that any significant proposed capital investments represent a smart commercial decision.

Once you make a major investment in a piece of machinery or a brand-new building you are saddled with those assets, and the costs associated with them, for years to come, whether or not the investment ultimately turns out to have been a good decision with the benefit of hindsight.

So, make sure your investment appraisal has a good margin of safety. That will help investors and lenders understand your planned investment is a game-changing opportunity, and one worth shooting for.

Financial Projections: The numbers that matter

Some people think the Financial section comes a bit late in a business plan. But business plans are put together in this sequence for a reason.

Until you know the strategies you intend to follow, the customers you want to attract, the costs of running your operations and all the other aspects we have covered in your business plan so far, you can't possibly have any solid basis for constructing financial projections for your business.

The only possible exception might be where you expect next year to be exactly like this year in every respect.

Experience tells me that is almost always an unwise assumption. But even if you might occasionally get away with that, the likelihood is you will miss opportunities to propel your business forward which the discipline of creating a business plan would have forced you to think through.

As we mentioned earlier, although the Financial section appears towards the end of your business plan document, when investors and lenders review your business plan, they are likely to read your Executive Summary then head straight for the Financial section.

So, although this appears towards the back of your business plan document, investors and lenders are likely to read this section fairly early in their review process. Take particular care that the Executive Summary flows clearly and cleanly into the Financial section especially if you wrote one several days, or even weeks, before you wrote the other.

When reviewing the Financial section of your business plan, investors and lenders will look both forwards at your future plans and backwards at what you've achieved in the past to give them a guide.

Again, credibility is key.

If your sales were $100,000 last year and you are planning sales of $10million this year, you are inviting questions you had better have some very good answers for.

If you run a start-up, you will obviously only have future projections to go on. So you will have to leverage the track record and experience of your founders and management team to demonstrate credibility to investors and lenders.

But if you have been in business for a while, include as much past financial data as possible.

While historic results are not usually too much of a problem, sometimes business owners get concerned about the need to project future financial results, especially in conditions of uncertainty – after all, nothing is certain about the future, is it?

However, there is no need to worry. This should not be difficult if you have followed through each section in this Action Guide so far.

Think about it.

You know the products and services you intend to sell, the prices you're going to charge and the unit margins on each product.

You know who you intend to sell your products and services to, the cost of attracting the number of customers you need to reach your sales target, and the processes you will deploy to make those sales.

You know the personnel you need to deliver your product or service and therefore what they will cost in salaries and benefits.

You know the investments you need to make in facilities, capital equipment, IT or other assets and the cost of each.

Armed with all that information, your forward financial projections should be a relatively simple matter. Much of the information you need will just be extracted from the relevant chapter of this Action Guide.

Finalising your numbers

Although you will have worked out much of your financial plan already in the previous sections, there are two groups of costs which you probably won't have addressed by this point in the process.

However, they should be relatively easy to slot into the Financial section now.

The first category are those costs which don't impact at a product gross margin or operational management level, such as rent for your premises, business insurance and accounting fees.

Although you are coming at them relatively late in the process, these costs tend to be relatively simple to find the right numbers for.

If you want to know what your accounting charges for next year will be, just ask your accountant and they will tell you. If you need an estimate for next year's business insurance costs, just ask your broker and they will give you one. Once you have the answers you need, just drop them into your financial projections and you're done.

The second category is more complicated. This category is made up of the costs you can't work out until after you've done everything else.

For example, you can't calculate the projected interest charges on a revolving credit facility until after you've prepared your detailed cash flow projection because until you've done that, you won't be able to see what use you're likely to make of the credit facility at your disposal.

Equally, you can't work out the tax charge to include in your income statement and cash flow until you know what your estimated profit for the year is going to be.

This second category, where you don't know what the costs will be until relatively late in the process, tend to be charges for which appropriate professional advice should be sought.

Unless you operate in a jurisdiction with simple, flat rate taxes (which virtually nobody does) working out your business tax liability is not a task which should be undertaken lightly by someone without an appropriate professional qualification.

Again, don't be put off seeking that advice. If you present a well-organised and well-ordered plan, which you will if you follow the methodology set out in this Action Guide, your accountant or financial advisor will be able to give you the answers you need relatively easily.

Unless you have unusual personal circumstances, their input will not normally be expensive.

However, the right professional advice can make a huge difference to your tax bill. So it's worth taking the time…and investing a small amount of money…to get it right and make sure you don't end up having some uncomfortable conversations with the tax authorities next time it's your turn for an audit.

Should you hire a financial advisor?

This is one part of the business planning process where, unless you have the skills yourself, or someone in-house does, you might find it easier, faster and ultimately cheaper to get a CPA or appropriate external advisor to pull together your financial projections in a format, and to a level of detail, investors and lenders expect to see.

There is no great mystery to pulling those numbers together, and of course you can learn how to do it yourself. But getting someone else to do it for you in return for a relatively small amount of money can shave weeks or months off the timescale you would otherwise need to create your business plan.

Because they have done this sort of work hundreds of times before, your CPA or financial advisor will blast through the job in no time.

Sometimes business owners are anxious about the cost of using external advisors. But if you have done the work in the earlier chapters, this should not be expensive.

You are essentially giving your CPA a script, with much of the work already done. They just need to slot those numbers into their financial modelling software to produce your projected income statement, balance sheet and cash flow without too much trouble.

Where it does become expensive to use external advisors is when business owners have not followed the process outlined in the earlier chapters of this Action Guide.

That's because getting your CPA to do the thinking for you about different marketing approaches, sales metrics and staffing requirements is an extremely expensive way to gobble through a couple of weeks of their time at several hundred dollars an hour.

Leaving aside the cost element, CPAs tend not to be the best people to do sales and marketing research in any event. And, in fairness, you can't expect them to know how businesses in your sector operate as well as you do.

So don't outsource the thinking that underpins your business plan to a CPA or financial advisor, but by all means outsource the doing...the turning of the "script" you developed through the process outlined in this Action Guide into the financial projections investors and lenders expect to see.

Finally, even though this is the Financial section, don't forget that "a picture can paint a thousand words".

Where appropriate use colorful charts, graphs, and charts to help drive your points home. Even sophisticated professional investors and lenders tire of seeing rows upon rows of figures on spreadsheets all day long.

A splash of color or a chart that makes an important point impactfully can make it much easier to get your perspective across and attract the funding you need.

One of the main purposes of a good business plan, aside from the benefits it brings to your business, is to make it easy for investors and lenders to say "yes".

An impactful presentation of your financial numbers is a great way to make that "yes" as easy as it's ever going to be.

Financial Projections: Must-haves

Copies of the full documents should be in the Appendix section later in your business plan document. In the Financial section, you should pull out the key numbers, KPIs and performance stats from your:

- Income statements
  Ideally for the last 2-3 years, with forecasts at least a similar period into the future.

- Balance sheets
  For the same time periods as your income statements.

- Cash flow statements
  For the same time periods as your income statements and balance sheets.

- Detailed operating budgets
  For last year, the current year and next year as a minimum.

- Unusual terms
  Any relevant accounts receivable and payable information, such as any unusual or onerous credit terms eg extended credit agreements or sales made on a "sale or return" basis.

- Revenue recognition policy
  Especially if your business sells longer term commitments, such as ongoing service contracts, take special care to outline your revenue recognition policies. There are a range of special rules your CPA can advise you on but, for example, if you sell a three-year agreement at $100,000 a year, do you book that as a $300,000 sale at the time you sign the contract or $100,000 each year for three years?

  The precise answer will depend on your individual circumstances, and you should seek appropriate professional advice. But enough lawsuits have been fought over precisely this issue in the past that you would be best advised to spell out exactly what you do up-front if your business enters long-term commitments with clients.

- <u>Debt repayment schedule</u>
  Details of any existing debt you carry, including the repayment schedules, dates when your existing debt will be cleared and the amount of any unused existing facilities.

  Lenders and investor will want to be certain you are able to meet your ongoing repayments and any capital repayments due under existing financial commitments without impacting on their interests in the business.

Objective: Financial section

Most of your business plan should be about persuasion, but the Financial section should be "just the facts" in as clear and simple a way as possible.

In large measure, your Financial section should be drawing on the work done in previous sections. It should be really clear how, for example, your marketing expenses in the Sales and Marketing section flow into the financial model, or how your product profitability from your Products and Services section feeds through into your projections.

You won't win the funding you're looking for in the Financial section, but it's easy to lose it here by doing the equivalent of what a salesperson would call "talking yourself out of a sale"…where the client is happy to buy, but you drone on for so long they lose interest.

You are closing things down here. You either made your sale or you didn't in the preceding sections.

If investors and lenders didn't believe you then, they won't believe you now.

By the same token, if they thought your basic ideas were good but they flip into a wildly unrealistic financial plan you can kiss your hopes of securing their financial support goodbye.

So, don't introduce new concepts you haven't covered before or re-open a debate you went through in a previous section. Be clear that you have already taken the decisions in the earlier sections and all you're doing in the Financial section is recording the results of those decisions in monetary terms.

You want investors and lenders to be able to flip back to earlier sections and go "yes, I see where that number came from" as they work their way through the Financial section so they realise your whole plan hangs together as it should.

Funding Request: What you need

Whether you are looking for external funding or not it is still worth giving this section a quick review as it could highlight where things might get a little tight financially and draw your attention to the key financial numbers you will want to keep a close eye on.

Preparing an annual business plan is a great discipline to get into either way.

However, if you are looking for funding – whether that's a loan, an equity injection, or some combination of the two – this is clearly an important section of your business plan.

Think long term

Your mindset in this section should be on the next 3-5 years, not the next few months.

That is especially true because a lot of financial decisions which sound like an "easy way out" in the short term turn out to be phenomenally expensive in the long term.

Financial institutions are well aware of this, which is why they sell their most profitable products the way they do – today's easy decision is tomorrow's financial millstone.

By keeping your focus out 3-5 years into the future, you are more likely to spot the little tricks financial institutions sometimes play with things like rate resets, inflation adjustments, repayment schedules and termination fees, potentially save yourself a fortune in the process.

Fundamentally, though, this section is your "ask".

Here you set out the financing you are looking for, on what terms, and over what period.

That is not to say you're going to get what you ask for. But if you don't ask, it's even less likely you'll get what you want.

So be bold. Be confident. Believe in yourself and ask for what you need.

Topics to cover in this section of your business plan include:

- The amount of funding you need right now.

- Funding you will need within a three-to-five-year planning horizon at least, including any additional funding you might require during that period, even if you don't need it right now.

- The type of funding you're seeking (loan, equity investment, etc).

- The indicative terms you're looking for, such as loan duration, the amount of equity on offer to an investor and so on. There will obviously be some negotiation around the final terms, but there is no harm in setting out your thoughts here, at a high level.

   If you are only prepared to give a 5% stake, but your investor only takes majority stakes in businesses they invest in, you can both save a lot of time if it's clear up-front that you're not a good match for one another instead of skirting around the issue or avoiding it altogether.

- Especially for equity investors, consider and illustrate the dilution effect of future fundraising rounds if you already have plans for those.

  In advance of doing a deal at some point in the future, this can only be illustrative, but being clear with investors at the outset that a further fundraising round will be required in a couple of years can minimise the chances of businesses and their investors falling out along the way.

Giving security

This is only an issue if you're looking for debt finance as the whole point of investors buying a percentage of your business is that they are accepting some degree of risk in the short term in return for the chance of a much bigger payday at some point in the future.

But if you are looking for debt finance, at some point in the process it is almost inevitable potential lenders will ask what security or collateral you would be prepared to put up in return for their funding.

In general, though, do not offer security at this stage. There is no need. Providers of debt finance, like banks, will be fast enough to ask for security or collateral if they want it.

While you may ultimately have to do something, don't give away any security you don't have to and certainly be extremely wary about giving security against your family home or investments which were intended to fund your retirement.

If you give security for anything, of course it should hurt a bit if that security is called in. The whole point of giving a lender security is to make sure you feel some pain if the project isn't successful. Lenders think that keeps you focused on paying back what you owe them.

But it shouldn't hurt too much. If your security is called in, you should not be left destitute. Any lender who is pushing for terms that would leave you homeless if your business plan doesn't work isn't a lender you want to be working with.

The only exception to the general rule of not offering security is for real estate purchases, where it is normal for banks and other lenders to take security over the asset their loan has been used to purchase. You may have no other option in practice because every provider insists on the same terms.

That apart, avoid giving security if you possibly can.

Yes, it makes your lender more secure but, by definition, it makes you less secure because there is a chance...however tiny...that your lender might call that security in one day.

And even if you have absolutely no choice at the start, try to negotiate terms so that after a certain amount of time or on achieving certain financial milestones, any security is released back to you without charge.

If you make all your loan payments on time for five years, for example, that might be reasonable. Or if you pay off 50% of the initial loan advance so the lender's risk in the event of a default is considerably reduced.

They might say no, but there is no harm in asking. There's only upside for you if they say yes and agree to release any security once they are happy the plan they bought into is going in the right direction.

Making sure your funding aligns with your business needs

Clearly, most of your funding "ask" will be driven by the financial section of your business plan, in which you should already have highlighted factors like seasonal dips in cash flow, the timing of stage payments for major investments in new plant and machinery, and so on.

The nature of the peaks and troughs in your cash flow projections will also make a difference to the type of financial support you ask for.

A highly seasonal business is likely to need a different financial product than one which has relatively steady demand throughout the year. A business making a large up-front investment in new machinery will have different financing needs from a business with much lower capital investment requirements.

You will have mentioned features like the seasonality in your business or your capital investments planned earlier in the business plan, but don't bank on people remembering what they read previously. Use this section as another opportunity to sell your business and your future plans to investors and lenders.

Remind them why getting involved in your business is a great opportunity for them. Remind them of the benefits to them of embarking on a long-term partnership which will grow as your business grows.

Don't repeat every detail but repeat the highlights. Remind them why you are looking for them to invest in your business and make sure your business appears in its best light.

It is also perfectly OK to refer readers back to the earlier section in which you explained all that in more detail.

Don't make the mistake of thinking this section is all about numbers.

At the same time as you present your "ask" you need to help investors and lenders answer the question they're quite reasonably going to have in mind... "what's in it for me?"

"What's in it for me?"

All investors and lenders want to be at least relatively sure they are going to get their money back, so give them lots of reasons to believe they will.

Do not make things up or be over-optimistic. But give investors and lenders as much confidence as you legitimately can that this will be a great investment for them, while being open about any risk factors.

Investors and lenders want to work with professional people who know their stuff. This is your chance to demonstrate you are one of those people.

Investors and lenders want to forge long-term relationships with good people who make their payments on time and don't cause any trouble. Show them you are one of those people.

And all investors and lenders want the bragging rights of their "ah, yes, I supported them when they were starting out, but just look at them now!" stories.

Don't be frightened to ask for the support you need. But don't forget to remind investors and lenders of all the good things you'll do for them in return.

That's how you make it easy for them to say "yes" to you.

Finally, make sure this section is tailored to the audience you're taking it to.

Your CPA or other advisor can help with this, but if you are approaching a handful of banks for a loan, this section might look a little different than if you were approaching a handful of venture capital folk to take an equity stake in your business.

There is a temptation to try and cover all the bases and only have one plan which you use with everyone. But I would caution against that as it can make you look a little unfocused and unstructured, or someone who's just hawking the same plan to all-comers.

It's like sending an identical CV out blindly to every job you see advertised. That approach isn't likely to get you many interviews, and neither is a single business plan that tries to be all things to all people.

It is, however, relatively easy to tailor the same basic plan, with just a tweak to this section and some revised wording along the way, and present something to different audiences which looks like it was written just for them.

You might even find that some lenders or investors make you use an in-house template for your business plan to help them review and compare multiple applications.

That's fine too – it's always worth asking if there's a particular format lenders or investors would like you to use. If they do, just give that to your CPA and ask them to complete it for you.

However, I would still complete this section of your business plan document regardless, as that's going to provide your CPA with a "script" they can translate into the format your lender or investor has asked for.

And it's also your opportunity to tell your story once again - one thing I can guarantee is that no lender or investor will ever have a section in their template which says "tell me all the great things about your business and this proposal so you can make it easy for me to say yes".

My advice would be to complete this section whether investors or lenders ask for it or not, and always to send in a complete business plan even if they ask you to use a template of their own design.

Just because they haven't asked you for a list of all the great things you have planned, doesn't mean you can't tell them anyway.

Remember, your business plan is a selling document. Make it easy for your investor or lender to say "yes".

Funding Request: Must-haves

- <u>Funding required</u>
  The amount of funding you're looking for over the next three to five years, using a summary of your cash flow projection to show the peaks and troughs in the need for funding, where appropriate.

- <u>Type of funding</u>
  What type of funding are you seeking (loan, equity investment, convertible bonds, etc)?

- <u>Terms</u>
  Your indicative terms, such as loan duration or the amount of equity you are prepared to offer investors.

- <u>Future fundraising rounds</u>
  If you have further fundraising rounds planned which will dilute the equity investor who come on board in this round, be clear about the funding you are likely to need, the

timescale and the effect of any dilution.

- <u>Options and convertible securities outstanding</u>
  Give clarity about any outstanding options which are convertible into shares in the business, such as share incentives offered to your senior management team or existing loans which carry the option to convert some or all of that loan to equity under certain predetermined situations.

Objective: Funding Request

Continuing the model of thinking about your business plan as a selling document, now you're going for the close.

Don't start opening up any debates you don't have to. Bring the conversation in nice and tight and ask for the sale.

Be clear about how much funding you want, and on what terms. That is all you need to get across here.

Expect negotiation, of course, but start the conversation by being clear about what you want.

Risk Analysis: What could go wrong (and right)?

The very final section in your business plan, before the Appendix section with copies of any supporting documents, should be the Risk Analysis section.

To be clear, I am not referring to the common...and largely pointless...Risk Management Plan exercise big companies are fond of and which you might have seen, or even participated in, before.

They are usually an excruciating attempt to score a range of random events that might and might not happen on a risk scale (typically scored on a 1-5 scale depending on the likelihood of that risk) and then multiplying that score by an assessment of the severity of the risk, should it come to fruition (again usually on a 1-5 scale).

The thinking goes that events which score 25 (5 x 5) are big risks that you should be doing something about and risks that score 1 (1 x 1) are risks which require very little attention.

The trouble with this sort of Risk Management Plan is three-fold:

1. Often the biggest risks are overlooked completely.

    I can't tell you the number of risk management plans I've seen that don't consider the impact of common occurrences like the business's largest customer not dealing with them anymore, or the impact on their own revenues of strike actions by their own staff or the staff of a key supplier.

2. The scoring is hilariously inconsistent, depending on who has completed which element of the plan.

I have seen the sort of event that would get your operating licence pulled by a regulator scored as a 5 and the risk of a brief outage on the telephone system scored at 25, leading to a lot of time managing the phone system and very little time spent addressing the risks that could get a business's operating licence terminated.

3. Having identified a risk beyond a threshold (10 points, say) every risk is supposed to have a risk management plan attached, showing all the things the business is doing to minimise either the risk of it happening in the first place, or minimising the severity of the risk should the event materialise despite the business's best efforts.

    This consumes so much management time that any benefits from minimising the risks are often swallowed up by so much bureaucracy that the net benefit to the business, in the end, is little or nothing.

It is important to say I am not against risk management. I am just against the way it's usually done, especially in large corporate environments. I rarely see a risk management plan which isn't, in large measure, pretty worthless.

However, the sort of risk analysis we are talking about in this section is not the corporate bureaucrat's pointless box-ticking paradise.

Frankly, unless you work in a sector with critical health and safety issues to manage or a regulatory environment which means you won't have a business unless you have one of those traditional risk management plans, your investors and lenders won't be that interested in, for example, how you manage the HR risks of someone suing for unfair dismissal (a common "risk" identified in those corporate-style plans).

They just expect you to run a proper business and manage those events as a matter of course, taking sensible steps to minimise risks where possible and economically rational. The last thing investors and lenders want to get involved in assessing the likelihood that your HR Department can do its job properly.

What investors and lenders are very interested in, though, is a risk analysis of your business performance – sometimes also called a sensitivity analysis (the term I prefer, to separate this sort of worthwhile exercise from box-ticking corporate bureaucrats' interpretation of the term "risk analysis").

Purpose of risk analysis (or sensitivity analysis)

We are right at the tail end of your business plan now. If investors and lenders have read this far, they are most definitely interested in your business and believe what they have to offer would be a good fit for your needs.

But there is one question they will still have in their minds... "well, that all sounds very nice in theory, but what happens if something goes wrong?".

This is why, right from the start of this Action Guide, I've been encouraging you to think about the 1-2-3 Method, where you look at what might happen if events don't go exactly according to plan...either on the downside or if things turn out much better than you ever dared hope.

Business owners often consider the implications of undershooting their business plan far more deeply than they consider what might happen if they knocked their plan out the park.

But if events turn strongly in your favour, you might even need some additional short-term funding.

If that's the case, it's much smarter to highlight that possibility at this stage so you can agree some headroom on your facility upfront instead of scrabbling around in a panic trying to stitch a short-term solution together if things go unexpectedly well.

Perhaps you're running an advertisement that's going really well, but it takes three months to sign up a customer after they respond to your advertisement.

The smart thing to do isn't to stop running the advertisement when you've spent your budget. It's to get more funding so you can run that advertisement over and over, so you grow even faster.

Three months from now, you will be able to recycle the additional income from the extra sales back through to finance your advertising again, but you might have a cash flow gap to manage in the three months between now and then.

Just be upfront about that...and also about why that should be a great strategy which your investors and lenders should want to support.

The Risk Analysis (or Sensitivity Analysis) section of your business plan is more about bringing together the points you have already explored in the previous section of the plan than doing anything new, so it should not require a huge amount of fresh work.

However, is it more helpful to give investors and lenders a view of all the potential "ups and downs" in one place than expect them to root through your business plan one section at a time to make a running total of what the different sensitivities might be and making their own estimates of the financial consequences of each.

The other reason for putting a separate Risk Analysis or Sensitivity Analysis section in your business plan is that there may be some risks or sensitivities which have not come up explicitly in the business planning process so far. You should highlight those in this section too.

Perhaps the lease is due up on your premises in 18 months' time, and while you are confident the lease will be renewed on the advantageous terms you enjoy today, you need to recognise that might not happen for all sorts of reasons outside your control.

Maybe a key member of staff is going to retire in two years' time and there is a succession plan to manage between now and then.

Perhaps a key customer contract is up for renewal in 12 months' time, and while you are confident it will be renewed, you need to recognise it might not be, despite your best efforts.

Events like those are unlikely to have had much prominence elsewhere in your business plan, so mention them here, if their impact on your bottom line is significant.

The risks or sensitivities to highlight

For business planning purposes, there is no need to explore every potential risk in this section, however minor.

This is the place for risks which would have a major impact on your sales, operating costs, profitability, or cash flow.

The definition of "major" will depend on your business, but I usually suggest having a threshold, such as a 5-10% impact on one or more of those metrics, before putting the event into the Sensitivity Analysis section of your business plan.

That is also a good way to make sure the unhelpful sort of corporate risk analysis mentality doesn't start creeping in, where pages and pages of badly scored risks get listed – so many that everyone gives up the will to live no more than a couple of pages in.

If you have annual revenues of $10 million and there is a risk that something could go wrong with a maximum cost impact of $10,000, it shouldn't have a place in the Sensitivity Analysis (or Risk Analysis, if you prefer) section of your business plan.

That's not to say the event isn't important in its own right, and that some manager or other shouldn't be keeping an eye on it and trying to make sure that risk never comes to fruition.

It's just that in the context of a strategic business plan, a $10,000 potential downside for a $10 million business is almost certainly not strategic enough to make the cut.

And don't just focus on events going against you.

Consider, for example, the impact of sales coming in 20% higher than forecast – could you get the skilled people you need to capitalise on that opportunity at short notice? And, if so, at what cost?

The recent pandemic was a great example of this. When stores were locked down so nobody could visit in person to make a purchase, online sales skyrocketed.

Most major retailers had sufficiently robust websites that placing the orders generally wasn't an issue but getting orders to customers was. The retailers didn't employ enough drivers or have enough trucks to make deliveries, because previously people just turned up at their stores to make a purchase.

As it happens, the need for drivers was less of an issue, because there were plenty of people who would have worked in the (now closed) stores. They could be redirected to delivery work instead.

But finding enough trucks was much trickier. Dealers and truck manufacturers only carry so much stock and some of them had their factories or dealerships closed or on short time working through the pandemic too.

That's why sales skyrocketing isn't always the "nice problem to have" people often tell you it is.

For some businesses...those who haven't done the sort of analysis we're talking about here...a spike in sales can sound the death-knell for them instead of opening the door on a whole new world of opportunities.

And all because they frittered away too much of their risk management effort on risks that didn't really matter or because they never considered that doing much better than expected can bring as many, if not more, challenges than when events go against you.

Focus on the net impact

Once you identify the significant risks and sensitivities in your business, the next step is to consider whether you can take action to offset the impact of those events.

Some of the scenarios you model, even if the impact looks dramatic at headline level, will turn out to have little or no impact on your overall financial results.

For example, if your sales are down by 10% but your wage costs (perhaps 70-80% of sales value in a people-centric services business) could be squeezed down by 15% in reasonably short order, the net impact on your bottom line and cash flow would be close to zero.

It can go the other way, of course, where small percentage changes have a significant bottom line impact.

When I worked in the printing industry, our paper costs were typically 50% of our selling price value, and the sector's net margins at the time were around 2% of sales.

That means if the cost of paper, which was determined on the commodity markets, went up by just 5%, our net margin would be completely wiped out. A 5% fluctuation in price might not sound like much, but the net impact on the bottom line would have been significant.

That's why I prefer the term sensitivity analysis to risk analysis for this section of your business plan.

Sensitivity analysis is about is understanding which issues will have the largest net impact on your business. In some areas of your business, the impact of even a relatively small percentage change can be huge. So, don't just focus on your biggest headline risks.

Typically, there is only a small number of genuinely significant sensitivities in any business, and many fewer than you might think if you have only ever seen one of those corporate box-ticking style risk management exercises.

What you are trying to highlight for investors and lenders is the ***net*** impact on your business because ultimately that's the impact they are trying to understand.

Sales down by $1 million and costs down by $1 million has a net bottom line impact of zero.

Of course, sales being down by $1 million is almost certainly unwelcome, but if you can quickly reduce your costs by a similar amount, then that is actually a significant positive for investors and lenders who will be more comfortable making an investment in your business.

If you can scale costs up and down quickly, easily, and inexpensively as sales go up and down, then your biggest bottom-line risks are not your sales numbers, but something else. Other metrics might well be much more critical to your financial performance than even a significant reduction in sales would be.

You need to work out a range of scenarios to understand what those sensitivities might be. Those scenarios are different for every business, but there is always something.

Presentation to investors and lenders

Part of the reason for working out a range of scenarios is that you want to give investors and lenders confidence that you have thought ahead of the game.

You want to be able to reassure investors and lenders that, while there could be some issues which might look problematic on the surface, in practice they are not the source of any significant concern for investors and lenders as a result of the plans you have put in place.

That will help you manage their expectations in the future. And, of course, it will help you manage your business because now you know which metrics will have the greatest impact on your overall financial performance, you can stay close to them.

The instinct of most investors and lenders would be to start panicking if sales came in $1 million short. But if you can help them understand that you can cut your costs by the same amount, quickly, easily and inexpensively, they'll be a lot easier to handle in the event the sales performance bounces around a little.

So it's worth spending some time educating investors and lenders and showing them, at a very high level, that there are a number of areas where, even if thing go wrong, you have plans in hand to sure you counteract that movement either completely or in large part.

Having told them what not to worry about, you should then focus in on what they should worry about.

In most businesses there are only a small number of these. But try to keep the list of sensitivities down to no more than five or ten key issues if at all possible, ideally ranked down from the biggest potential net impact on your bottom line down to the smallest.

Don't be tempted to do what a lot of risk management plans do and split them down by internal departments, starting with the risks from the HR Department, perhaps, followed by the risks from the Marketing Department, and so on.

That's an unhelpful format for investors and lenders as they have to trawl through the whole document to find what the key issues are and keep referring backwards and forwards to see if this risk from the Logistics Department has a bigger or smaller impact than another risk from the Quality Assurance Department.

Just set them out in rank order, biggest to smallest, ideally no more than five to ten of them.

If you think you have more than 10 major risks in your business, you might need to recalibrate your definition of what a major risk is. There are plenty of things you might hope aren't going to happen, but if the financial impact is small or non-existent, investors and lenders...in the nicest possible way...just don't care.

A helpful format

A good format for this section, after a preamble to explain the basis on which you have selected your key risks or sensitivities, is to set your key risks out in a table.

In the first column, explain what each individual risk or sensitivity is and what level of fluctuation you are considering in this analysis (sales down by 10%, minimum wage costs up by 20%, etc).

In the second column show how much your bottom line (or cash flow if that is a more significant factor in your business plan) would be impacted by a difference of that magnitude.

In the third column highlight the action you are taking to minimise the impact of that event, were it to happen.

And finally, in a fourth column, show the net impact on your bottom line or cash flow, on the assumption those mitigating actions have the desired effect.

To build on the example used earlier in this section, you might show the impact on your bottom line of sales being short by $1 million, then explain that you have a very flexible workforce which means you can quickly scale down your workforce to make sure the net impact on your bottom line is zero, or somewhere close to it.

Whatever the impact on your business from the range of scenarios you explore, don't try to underestimate the impact on your business, thinking it makes you look good.

Professional investors and lenders know there is no such thing as a risk-free proposition.

What they want to understand is whether or not they're dealing with an amateur who hasn't fully thought through the consequences of their business plan.

If you identify the sensitivities with a significant impact on your business's financial performance and highlight what you are doing to keep on top of whatever those key issues might be, professional investors and lenders will be fine with your proposal.

Again, if they're not, that's a sign you're dealing with an amateur lender or investor and they can often be more trouble than they're worth. Professionals always understand.

They might not want to shoulder extreme risks at the price you are prepared to pay, but that's a different issue altogether, and an illustration of why it's important to deal with lenders or investors who share your risk appetite.

If you ask your local bank to fund a speculative diamond mine in a remote corner of Africa which is frequently laid destitute by civil war, don't be too surprised if they turn down your funding request. There are people who will fund those projects, just not at the same rates you would get from your local bank.

Neither is right or wrong. They are both the right funding solution for the right project. Your job here is to find a lender or investor with a risk appetite that matches your own once you have explained the key risks and sensitivities in your business plan.

Finally

Remember, this section should not be a whole new piece of complex work.

If you have followed through with the 1-2-3 Method and highlighted the risks and sensitivities in each section as recommended in this Action Guide, this section is largely about collating in one place issues you have already highlighted elsewhere.

Feel free to reference any scenarios listed in this section back to a more in-depth discussion in the relevant section (marketing, financial, etc) earlier in your business plan. You can also refer any significant risks or sensitivities discussed in those earlier sections to the Risk Analysis section here both to demonstrate the robustness of your plan and to minimize repetition.

Unless you run nuclear power stations or an aeroplane manufacturing business, the Risk Analysis or Sensitivity Analysis section should be a short, punchy section and one of the briefest in your entire plan.

You should only highlight the small number of absolutely key issues which you will be tracking, managing and reporting on to investors and lenders on a regular basis to make sure your bottom line and cash flow is protected, should the worst happen.

Objective: Risk Analysis

You don't want to spook the horses here. This section is more in the nature of objection-handling, to continue the sales metaphor from the previous section, than anything else.

Even if they like your plan so far, investors and lenders will be thinking about any potential downsides to your proposal. That is entirely natural and, after all, it's what they get paid to worry about.

As long as you demonstrate you've thought about a range of likely potential adverse events and have a plan to minimise their impact on your business should the worst happen, you're well on your way to dismantling any objections investors and lenders are likely to have.

Appendix

In all the previous sections, you have been trying to paint a compelling picture of what your business is like and where it's headed.

You needed to provide investors and lenders with enough information to help them grasp your vision, but not so much information that you bogged them down and made it harder for you to tell an impactful story.

Every business plan should have an appendix. This is where you provide all the extra details investors and lenders will need without disrupting the flow of your narrative in the earlier sections.

The appendix section should contain copies of all the supporting documents which substantiate the claims you made and facts you have cited in the previous sections, such as the size of the market you're targeting or details from the financial records of your competitors.

The Appendix is normally split into numbered sub-sections for ease of reference. For example, earlier in your business plan you might say "For last year's audited accounts, please see Appendix 7".

If the reader wants to look at that information in more detail, they simply refer to the relevant part of the appendix.

This isn't an exhaustive list, and depending on the nature of your business, you might have a range of other information in here too. However, these items are commonly found in business plan appendices:

- Previous years' full audited accounts

- Credit histories

- Regulatory permits to operate (if appropriate)

- Photographs, engineering drawings of your products, architects' plans

- Legal documents, such as leases or key contracts

- Any licenses you need

- Registered patents, trademarks and copyrights held by the company relevant to your business plan proposal

- Significant legal contracts relevant to your future plans, eg a distributorship agreement in a foreign country

- Anything else that might be relevant, and certainly anything else you have mentioned in the plan itself.

  Professional investors and lenders will ask for copies of any important documents you mention anyway, so you might as well demonstrate your professionalism by saying, for example, "A copy of our revenue recognition policy can be found in Appendix 9" and include a copy there for them to review.

Objective: Appendix

This section is purely concerned with providing evidence to back up whatever you said earlier in your business plan.

If you claim your financial performance over the past three years has been exceptional, put a copy of your audited accounts in here to show you weren't making it up.

If you claim to have a patent, trademark, or other intellectual property protection for a key aspect of your product or service, include a copy of the official certification here.

If a major part of the forecast revenues in your business plan represents the revenues which you expected to come from an exclusive 10-year contract with Harrods, put a copy of your contract with them here.

The purpose of this section is not to introduce new information investors and lenders haven't seen before, but to provide an overwhelming body of evidence to demonstrate you can back up every claim you made in your plan so investors and lenders can be confident enough to give you the support you need.

Do not think for a moment investors and lenders will read every element in detail, but they will have a close look at elements which particularly interest them and they will take great comfort, even for the bits they only glance at, from the weight of evidence you put forward to back up your claims.

You establish enormous amounts of credibility with this section of your business plan. Don't miss an opportunity to reinforce with investors and lenders that you are the sort of person they can have complete confidence in.

Time to Build Your Dream!

Yes, creating a business plan takes a bit of work. Like any other professional job worth doing well, it takes time to create a compelling plan that convinces others to support your vision. But it's time well spent.

Creating a business plan gives you incredible clarity about your business and unique insights into what it will take for your business to succeed.

The business planning process pushes you to differentiate yourself from your competitors. It compels you to create a powerful marketing and sales plan. And it makes sure you know your financial numbers inside and out.

If you feel overwhelmed at the thought of trying to get everything done, just focus on getting one section done at a time.

Do one step, then the next, then the next. Before you know it, you will have completed your entire business plan.

And as you work on your business plan, keep the big picture in mind.

The reason you're doing all this work is so you can build your dream business.

The time you invest up front to create a thorough and compelling business plan will be repaid many times over when your business becomes wildly successful.

Don't wait any longer to create your business plan. Your dream business is just around the corner.

It's time to get to work!

The Most Important Reason to Create a Business Plan

For many people, all they want is a business plan.

A lender or investor has told them they need one, so they follow the steps in this book and write one. Job done; they move on to the next fire that needs putting out.

Of course, I wish them luck. But if that is the only reason you're preparing a business plan, you're missing a great opportunity for your business and yourself.

The real reason to prepare a business plan – and the reason you should prepare one every year whether you plan to raise any external funding or not – is that you now have a roadmap, a template for how you're going to create the business of your dreams and achieve everything you wanted to achieve out of life.

A business plan is not a stale document for your banker's filing cabinet or your investor's library. At least, not if you're doing it right.

A good business plan is like writing your autobiography, setting out your achievements, your major milestones in life and your legacy.

The only difference between a business plan and an autobiography is that you write your business plan up-front instead of 40 years after the event.

That is the real value of a business plan.

You get to write your own autobiography in advance.

You know where you're headed.

You know what needs to happen to get you there.

You know if you are veering off-course early enough to get things back on track before it becomes too expensive and too difficult.

And you know how you are going to ramp up your business when that potent combination of hard work, the focus a business plan brings, and a lucky break or two along the way means your business gets opportunities you never dared dream were possible for you.

Use your business plan to set your course, track your performance and achieve your dreams.

That is easier said than done, of course, so we have a variety of resources to help support you on that journey.

If you haven't already downloaded your free "fill in the blanks" business plan template, do that now. You can find it at:

www.TheBetterBusinessCompany.com/BPtemplate

We also offer a range of coaching solutions to support you on your path to writing your business plan and achieving your dreams. You can find all the details at:

www.TheBetterBusinessCompany.com/BPcoach

I hope to see you there.

In the meantime, I wish you, and your business, the very best of luck.

Alastair Thomson
Author: "How to Build a Better Business Plan"

Printed in Great Britain
by Amazon

17872856R00102